Careers in Focus

FORENSICS

Ferguson
An imprint of Infobase Publishing

Careers in Focus: Forensics

Copyright © 2010 by Infobase Publishing

Ferguson
An imprint of Infobase Publishing
132 West 31st Street
New York NY 10001

Library of Congress Cataloging-in-Publication Data

Careers in focus. Forensics.
    p. cm.
  Includes index.
  ISBN-13: 978-0-8160-8020-5 (hbk : alk. paper)
  ISBN-10: 0-8160-8020-8 (hbk : alk. paper) 1. Forensic sciences—Vocational guidance—Juvenile literature. 2. Criminal investigation—Vocational guidance—Juvenile literature.
  HV8073.8.C37 2010
  363.25023—dc22
                                        2009049674

Ferguson books are available at special discounts when purchased in bulk quantities for businesses, associations, institutions, or sales promotions. Please call our Special Sales Department in New York at (212) 967-8800 or (800) 322-8755.

You can find Ferguson on the World Wide Web at http://www.fergpubco.com

Text design by David Strelecky
Composition by Mary Susan Ryan-Flynn
Cover printed by Art Print, Taylor, PA
Book printed and bound by Maple Press, York, PA
Date printed: May 2010
Printed in the United States of America

10 9 8 7 6 5 4 3 2 1

Table of Contents

Introduction 1

Computer Forensics Specialists. 5

Crime Scene Investigators. 15

Criminalists 24

Fingerprint Analysts. 35

Fire Investigators 43

Forensic Accountants and Auditors 51

Forensic Anthropologists 62

Forensic Biologists 70

Forensic Botanists 79

Forensic Chemists. 86

Forensic Engineers 97

Forensic Entomologists. 109

Forensic Nurses 116

Forensic Odontologists. 126

Forensic Pathologists 136

Forensic Psychiatrists and Psychologists 147

Forensic Science Educators. 160

Forensic Science Laboratory Managers 171

Forensic Toxicologists 181

Questioned Document Examiners 189

Index 197

Introduction

The American Academy of Forensic Sciences defines forensic science as any science that is "used in public, in a court, or in the justice system." You are probably already familiar with forensic science after watching crime-oriented television shows such as *CSI: Crime Scene Investigation* but there is a lot more to the world of forensic science than crime scene investigation. And unlike TV shows, cases are not usually solved in an hour or two, but after days, weeks, or even years of investigation and careful, and sometimes monotonous, application of scientific techniques. There are opportunities in dozens of scientific fields—ranging from botany and chemistry, to dentistry and nursing, to accounting, psychiatry, and engineering.

Employment opportunities for forensic science professionals are available at crime laboratories; colleges and universities; law firms; insurance companies; local, state, and federal government agencies; and many other employers.

While a majority of careers in forensic science require at least a bachelor's degree, there are also opportunities for those with a high school diploma (crime scene investigators and fingerprint analysts) or some postsecondary training (fire investigators and forensic nurses). Other careers—such as forensic anthropologists and college professors—require a master's degree or a doctorate. Some positions—such as forensic pathologists, forensic odontologists, and forensic psychiatrists—require a medical degree.

Earnings for forensic science professionals range from $20,000 for new criminalists to more than $150,000 or more for forensic accountants and auditors, forensic pathologists, forensic toxicologists, and forensic science laboratory managers.

The U.S. Department of Labor predicts that employment for forensic science technicians will grow much faster than the average for all careers through 2016. Opportunities should be good for most forensic science professionals, although it is important to remember that many forensic science fields are very small and employ only a small number of workers. Those who are employed by local and state public safety departments should experience especially strong employment opportunities, although some government agencies may be under pressure to reduce staff because of budget shortfalls. Opportunities in certain professions may be better in the private sector, where funding is less of an issue. As with most careers, forensic science professionals with advanced education and considerable experience will have the best employment prospects.

A few of the articles in *Careers in Focus: Forensics* appear in Ferguson's *Encyclopedia of Careers and Vocational Guidance,* but have been updated and revised with the latest information from the U.S. Department of Labor, professional organizations, and other sources. Most have been created especially for this book.

The following paragraphs detail the sections and features that appear in the book.

The **Quick Facts** section provides a brief summary of the career including recommended school subjects, personal skills, work environment, minimum educational requirements, salary ranges, certification or licensing requirements, and employment outlook. This section also provides acronyms and identification numbers for the following government classification indexes: the Dictionary of Occupational Titles (DOT), the Guide for Occupational Exploration (GOE), the National Occupational Classification (NOC) Index, and the Occupational Information Network (O*NET)-Standard Occupational Classification System (SOC) index. The DOT, GOE, and O*NET-SOC indexes have been created by the U.S. government; the NOC index is Canada's career classification system. Readers can use the identification numbers listed in the Quick Facts section to access further information about a career. Print editions of the DOT (*Dictionary of Occupational Titles.* Indianapolis, Ind.: JIST Works, 1991) and GOE (*Guide for Occupational Exploration.* Indianapolis, Ind.: JIST Works, 2001) are available at libraries. Electronic versions of the NOC (http://www23.hrdc-drhc.gc.ca) and O*NET-SOC (http://online.onetcenter.org) are available on the Internet. When no DOT, GOE, NOC, or O*NET-SOC numbers are present, this means that the U.S. Department of Labor or Human Resources Development Canada have not created a numerical designation for this career. In this instance, you will see the acronym "N/A," or not available.

The **Overview** section is a brief introductory description of the duties and responsibilities involved in this career. Oftentimes, a career may have a variety of job titles. When this is the case, alternative career titles are presented. The **History** section describes the history of the particular job as it relates to the overall development of its industry or field. **The Job** describes the primary and secondary duties of the job. **Requirements** discusses high school and post-secondary education and training requirements, any certification or licensing that is necessary, and other personal requirements for success in the job. **Exploring** offers suggestions on how to gain experience in or knowledge of the particular job before making a firm educational and financial commitment. The focus is on what can be done while still in high school (or in the early years of college) to gain a better understanding of the job. The **Employers** section gives an overview of typical places of employment for the job. **Starting Out** discusses the best ways to land that first job, be it through the college career services office, newspaper ads, Internet employment sites, or personal contact. The **Advancement** section describes what kind of career path to expect from the job and how to get there. **Earnings** lists salary ranges and describes the typical fringe benefits. The **Work Environment** section describes the typical surroundings and conditions of employment—whether indoors or outdoors, noisy or quiet, social or independent. Also discussed are typical hours worked, any seasonal fluctuations, and the stresses and strains of the job. The **Outlook** section summarizes the job in terms of the general economy and industry projections. For the most part, Outlook information is obtained from the U.S. Bureau of Labor Statistics and is supplemented by information gathered from professional associations. Job growth terms follow those used in the *Occupational Outlook Handbook*. Growth described as "much faster than the average" means an increase of 21 percent or more. Growth described as "faster than the average" means an increase of 14 to 20 percent. Growth described as "about as fast as the average" means an increase of 7 to 13 percent. Growth described as "more slowly than the average" means an increase of 3 to 6 percent. "Little or no change" means a decrease of 2 percent to an increase of 2 percent. "Decline" means a decrease of 3 percent or more. Each article ends with **For More Information,** which lists organizations that provide information on training, education, internships, scholarships, and job placement.

Careers in Focus: Forensics also includes photographs, informative sidebars, and interviews with professionals in the field.

Computer Forensics Specialists

OVERVIEW

Computer forensics specialists are computer experts who examine computers and other technology for evidence of wrongdoing. They may also be known as *computer* or *cyber examiners*.

HISTORY

The late 1930s and early 1940s saw the dawning of the modern era of digital computers, with innovations continuing throughout the decades. As the power and potential of computers attracted more and more people over the years, computers soon appeared as an attractive means for mischief and illegal activity. In the 1970s students were able to figure out ways of accessing computer systems without proper authorization, and since then, computer-related offenses have only grown in frequency, sophistication, and criminal intent.

In the United States, the state of Florida passed the first law to deal with computer crimes—including gaining unauthorized access to computers or using computers to commit fraud—in 1978. On the federal level, the U.S. Federal Computer Fraud and Abuse Act was passed in 1984. Also that year, the Federal Bureau of Investigation's Magnetic Media Program—the predecessor to the FBI's current Computer Analysis and Response Team—was created.

As the frequency of computer crimes increased, law enforcement agencies responded with targeted programs to combat the crime in the 1980s and 1990s. International organizations such as the

International Association of Computer Investigative Specialists and the International Organization on Computer Evidence were created to assist in computer forensic endeavors, by standardizing methods and procedures for handling digital evidence and creating certification programs for computer forensic specialists. As technological advances were made with computer hardware and software, the computer forensic specialist's arsenal of tools expanded and improved to meet the challenges of combating cybercrime in the 21st century.

THE JOB

Computer forensics specialists search for evidence stored on computers of illegal activities such as credit-card fraud, identity theft, child pornography, terrorism, stealing trade secrets from a company or government agency, and illegally gaining access to, or "hacking," individual, corporate, or government computer systems.

Computers have taken the world by storm in recent decades and, while they have been a positive force for businesses, they have also opened up new avenues for criminal activity. Criminals may use computers to store data, such as credit card or personal-identification information, that they have acquired illegally through some other means. They may also use computers and their Internet connections as tools to commit crimes, attempting to connect to bank or other business networks, or the computers of private individuals, to pilfer confidential information. The use of "ghost terminals" is a common method of engaging in illegal activities; it involves a hacker connecting illegally to a computer that he or she does not own (such as one on a university campus) and then, from that computer, launching attacks on other networks and possibly storing data.

Computer forensics specialists use a technique called imaging to extract data from the computers of suspected criminals. It involves the creation of an exact copy of the data on a computer's hard drive, ensuring that the original data is not lost and preventing later accusations of data tampering. A type of imaging software called EnCase allows the extraction of data from different sources, including hard drives, Zip drives, PDAs, CD-ROMs, cell phones, and MP3 players. Another weapon in the arsenal is Vogon Forensic Software, which creates an exact copy of a drive and can also index the drive's contents very quickly, making it easier for investigators to search through the disk's contents. A feature of Microsoft Windows and other operating systems called Netstat lists all the connections one specific computer has with other computers. This can tell investi-

A computer forensics specialist with the Virginia State Police Computer Evidence Recovery Unit studies a hard drive. *(Steve Helber, AP Photo)*

gators if an individual has gained unauthorized access to another computer. Most of these types of software also have features that help specialists find data that may have been renamed and hidden in different areas of the hard drive in an attempt to prevent it from being discovered. Even with these tools, the task of investigating illicit computer activity requires a tremendous amount of patience and dedication.

There are also strict regulations that must be followed with regard to the collection of computer forensic evidence in order for that evidence to hold up in court. Computer forensics specialists must keep detailed records of their activities involving data collection. They must maintain what is referred to as the "chain of custody" of evidence in any given case; that is, through strict documentation of all work done from the first day of gathering information up to the presentation of the data in court. They must ensure and be able to prove that information taken from a computer has not been altered in any way (nothing added, nothing deleted) during the course of the investigation.

In addition to working in a law-enforcement capacity, computer forensics specialists are used by businesses to root out activity that may not necessarily be criminal but that may compromise the productivity of the business. For example, they may be called in to find out if an employee is using his or her company's computer to access adult Web sites, engage in peer-to-peer file transfers, or download and trade music and movies. Forensics specialists can recover deleted files, track network activity, and create reports that summarize the activities in which the employee has engaged. The role of the computer forensics specialist is also expanding into areas of prevention—figuring out ways to safeguard digital information to better protect it from being stolen or used illegally.

Computer forensics specialists employed by law enforcement agencies can be either civilian workers or sworn law enforcement officers who choose to work on special computer crime units.

REQUIREMENTS

High School

If you are a high school student and think you want to get into computer forensics, first and foremost you need to get involved in computer science classes. Hands-on experience is key and probably is what will help get you your first job. Spend time in the school computer lab, learn how computers work, and dabble with the latest technologies. Most of those employed in the field today began at a young age just playing around. What began as a hobby eventually turned into an enjoyable and challenging career.

You should also take classes in mathematics, science, and English. Speech classes will help you develop your oral communication skills, which will come in handy when testifying in court or during other legal proceedings.

Postsecondary Training

You will need a minimum of a bachelor's degree in computer science, information systems, or computer forensics to work in this field. Many computer forensics specialists go on to earn master's and even doctorates in order to become eligible for top positions. The American Academy of Forensic Sciences offers a list of colleges and universities that offer certificates and minors in computer forensics and related fields at its Web site (http://www.aafs.org). A more comprehensive list is available at http://www.e-evidence.info/education.html.

Once they are hired, computer forensics specialists add to their skills by participating in on-the-job training and attending seminars, workshops, and educational conferences, which are offered by professional associations such as the High Technology Crime Investigation Association and the International Association of Computer Investigative Specialists.

Certification or Licensing

The International Association of Computer Investigative Specialists offers the following voluntary certifications to computer forensics specialists: certified forensic computer examiner and certified electronic evidence collection specialist. The International Society of Forensic Computer Examiners offers the certified computer examiner designation. Contact these organizations for information on certification requirements.

The American College of Forensic Examiners offers the certified forensic consultant program, which provides an overview of the U.S. judicial system. This certification would be useful for computer forensics specialists who are required to testify in court. Contact the college for more information.

Computer forensics specialists who work as private investigators must often be licensed by the state in which they wish to practice. Contact your state's department of labor or department of licensing for more information on requirements in your state.

Other Requirements

To be a successful computer forensics specialist, you should be highly organized, have comprehensive knowledge of computer science, be detail oriented, have a curious personality, enjoy solving problems, have a very analytical mind, and be highly ethical. Other useful traits include effective time management skills, strong communication skills, and the ability to work as a member of a team.

It is not uncommon for those applying for computer forensics positions to have their backgrounds checked or at least have their list of references closely reviewed to make sure they are trustworthy.

EXPLORING

High school computer clubs and competitions allow you to experiment with computers. They are great places to design and implement systems and solutions in a nonthreatening atmosphere. You can also work with other students to get accustomed to working in teams.

Ask your computer science teacher or a career counselor to arrange an information interview with a computer forensics specialist. You should also visit Web sites and read publications about computer forensics. Here are a few book suggestions: *Computer Forensics For Dummies,* by Linda Volonino; *Computer Forensics and Cyber Crime: An Introduction,* 2nd ed., by Marjie T. Britz; and *Computer Forensics: Incident Response Essentials,* by Warren G. Kruse and

Jay G. Heiser. One other publication of interest is *Forensic Examination of Digital Evidence: A Guide for Law Enforcement,* from the U.S. Department of Justice. As the title indicates, it is geared toward professionals in the field, but reading through it will give you an excellent idea of the methods used in computer forensics investigations. Visit http://www.ncjrs.gov/pdffiles1/nij/199408.pdf to access the publication.

EMPLOYERS

Computer forensics specialists work for law enforcement agencies, military and government intelligence agencies, insurance companies, law firms, and private-security companies, and some of them are self-employed and work as consultants.

STARTING OUT

It is unlikely that someone fresh out of high school or college will get a job as a computer forensics specialist. Although education is important, experience is key in the field. This experience can be gained through work in computer security or from internships or other opportunities.

Applicants who are law enforcement officers typically have extensive experience with computer hardware and software as it relates to computer security and crime.

Many companies post job openings on their Web sites. Professional associations, such as the International High Technology Crime Investigation Association (http://www.htcia.org/classified/index.shtml), are also good sources of job leads.

ADVANCEMENT

Computer forensics specialists can move into supervisory or management positions and sometimes into executive positions (at private companies). With experience, a forensics specialist can become a consultant. Others become college professors. Police officers who work as computer forensics specialists advance by gaining rank, such as becoming detectives, sergeants, captains, and so on.

Computer forensics specialists may also choose to enter the related field of computer security. *Computer security specialists* are responsible for protecting a company or organization's computers and computer network, which can be accessed through the Internet, from intrusion by outsiders.

EARNINGS

There is no comprehensive salary information available for computer forensics specialists. The U.S. Department of Labor does provide information on computer scientists, not otherwise classified (a category that includes computer forensics specialists). The median salary for these professionals was $75,150 in 2008. Salaries ranged from less than $40,660 to $114,830 or more. In 2008 computer scientists working for the federal government earned a mean annual salary of $84,750.

Computer forensics specialists who work as consultants may be paid by the hour, by the day, or via a flat rate for tasks performed. Top consultants can earn $400 or more.

Benefits for full-time employees may include paid vacation, paid sick days, personal days, medical and dental insurance, and bonuses. Self-employed computer forensics specialists must provide their own benefits.

WORK ENVIRONMENT

Because computer forensics specialists work with computers and computers require a controlled atmosphere, the work environment is typically indoors in a well-lit, climate-controlled office or computer lab. Security specialists can expect to spend many hours sitting in front of a computer screen or working with other technology. Computer forensics specialists typically work 40 hours a week, with overtime. They may be required to travel to testify in court proceedings.

OUTLOOK

Employment for computer forensics specialists is expected to be strong during the next decade as more private companies and law enforcement agencies rely on these professionals to help solve crimes and investigate employee malfeasance and noncriminal violations of company policy.

FOR MORE INFORMATION

For information on forensic careers and education, contact
American Academy of Forensic Sciences
410 North 21st Street
Colorado Springs, CO 80904-2712
Tel: 719-636-1100
http://www.aafs.org

For information on forensic science and certification, contact
American College of Forensic Examiners
2750 East Sunshine Street
Springfield, MO 65804-2047
Tel: 800-423-9737
http://www.acfei.com

A professional organization for information security professionals, CSI provides education and training for its members. Visit its Web site for information on computer security and crime.
Computer Security Institute (CSI)
600 Harrison Street
San Francisco, CA 94107-1387
http://www.gocsi.com

For information on membership for college students and useful links, visit the association's Web site.
International High Technology Crime Investigation Association
3288 Goldstone Drive
Roseville, CA 95747-7167
http://www.htcia.org

For information on certification, contact
International Association of Computer Investigative Specialists
PO Box 2411
Leesburg, VA 20177-7699
Tel: 888-884-2247
http://www.iacis.com

For information on computer forensics investigations, contact
International Organization on Computer Evidence
http://www.ioce.org

For information on certification, contact
International Society of Forensic Computer Examiners
Tel: 615-236-1242
Email: info@isfce.com
http://www.isfce.com

INTERVIEW

Warren Kruse, CISSP, CFCE is the vice president of data forensics and analytics at Encore Discovery Solutions. He is also the coauthor of Computer Forensics: Incident Response Essentials. *Warren discussed his career and the field of computer forensics with the editors of* Careers in Focus: Forensics.

Q. What made you want to enter this career?

A. I was a police officer in New Jersey when businesses just started using personal computers. I thought it would benefit investigations by learning more about them so I started taking networking and computer forensics classes on my own. As it turns out the World Wide Web became a hit and computers started popping up in homes, schools, libraries, etc. The township manager at the time didn't want police officers working on computers so I vested my pension and started doing computer forensics and incident response full time.

Q. Can you tell me about Encore Discovery Solutions? What are your main and secondary job duties?

A. At Encore Discovery Solutions, our world-class team of discovery experts helps our clients identify and implement the right solution for any discovery or similar data-intensive challenge. We are an end-to-end provider, able to assist law firms and corporate law departments in each and every phase of the discovery process.

Encore Discovery Solutions is a leading global provider of high quality and innovative electronic and paper discovery solutions to Fortune 500 corporations and AmLaw 200 law firms. Ranked by the respected Socha-Gelbmann Electronic Discovery Survey as one of the nation's "Top 10 overall" electronic data discovery service providers, our focus on quality and client service is second to none. We currently host client data that equates to more than 20 times the volume of documents archived in the Library of Congress.

I am vice president of data forensics and analytics. My duties involve leading our team; in addition I act as an expert for our clients when needed. I also consult with our clients on best practices for preservation, collection, and searching electronically stored information.

Q. **What are some of the pros and cons of work in your field?**

A. Tons of pros: You are in demand, good pay, travel if you like that, but that could also be a con if you don't like to travel. I travel frequently and usually on short notice.

Q. **What is the future employment outlook for computer forensics specialists?**

A. More people are learning and getting into the field all the time. The future is good for people doing the work and also for people who can develop the next generation of software and tools we use. Hard drives are getting huge and the tools and methods we use today are quickly becoming obsolete so we need people to design, program, and implement new solutions. Computers are not going away, and unfortunately illicit use of computers is also not going to decline, so we need people doing computer forensics.

Q. **What advice would you give to high school students who are interested in this career?**

A. Study computers, law, and computer fraud and abuse. Look into police explorers or part-time positions in your local police department.

Q. **What have been some of your most rewarding or inter-esting experiences in your career?**

A. I've been to every state in the United States except for four, so I've been all over, seen amazing places, and met really inter-esting people. I've gone to Japan, Hong Kong, Saudi Arabia, climbed the pyramids in Cairo, been to Costa Rica, etc.—all for business. I did all the forensics [work] on a billion-dollar theft of intellectual property case, which literally made the cover of *Time* magazine and many other newspapers and magazines. I've worked on the Olympics security in Atlanta and Utah, where we collected and disseminated information on security and operational issues for all the private companies involved in the Olympics.

Crime Scene Investigators

OVERVIEW

Crime scene investigators are science professionals who go to the scene of a crime in order to collect and photograph relevant evidence, such as fingerprints, hairs, and bullet casings. Their work helps medical examiners, criminalists, and forensic scientists analyze, identify, and classify physical evidence relating to criminal cases. Crime scene investigators also work in laboratories and testify in court. They may be known as *forensic science technicians, evidence technicians, forensic investigators,* and *crime scene technicians.* In the past most crime scene investigators were police officers; today, they are more likely to be civilians working for police departments and other law enforcement agencies. There are approximately 12,000 crime scene investigators employed in the United States.

HISTORY

Physical evidence has been used to convict or absolve people of crimes for more than one thousand years. In approximately 1000 A.D. Quintilian, a Roman attorney, proved that the bloody palm prints left at a crime scene were not those of a blind man, who had been accused of his mother's murder. In 1248 a Chinese book, *The Washing Away of Wrong,* was published that helped investigators determine the difference between death by strangulation and death by drowning. But it was not until the 1800s that major medical and technological advances occurred that set the stage for the modern field of forensic science (which is only a little more than a century

Books to Read

Bertino, Anthony J. *Forensic Science: Fundamentals and Investigations*. Florence, Ky.: South-Western Educational Publishing, 2008.

Britz, Marjie T. *Computer Forensics and Cyber Crime: An Introduction*. 2d ed. Upper Saddle River, N.J.: Prentice Hall, 2008.

Camenson, Blythe. *Opportunities in Forensic Science Careers*. 2nd ed. New York: McGraw-Hill, 2008.

Evans, Colin. *The Casebook of Forensic Detection: How Science Solved 100 of the World's Most Baffling Crimes*. Hoboken, N.J.: Wiley, 1998.

Evans, Colin. *Murder Two: The Second Casebook of Forensic Detection*. Hoboken, N.J.: Wiley, 2004.

Funkhouser, John. *Forensic Science for High School Students*. Dubuque, Iowa: Kendall Hunt Publishing Company, 2005.

Hester, Ronald E., and Roy M. Harrison. (eds.) *Environmental Forensics*. London, U.K.: Royal Society of Chemistry, 2008.

old). These include the development of an accurate test for arsenic (a poison) in the blood (1836), experimentation on dead soldiers to determine the time of death (1839), steady improvements in the quality of microscopes and other investigative technologies, and the first identification of a criminal using fingerprints (1891).

In 1915 the International Association for Identification was founded by inspector Harry H. Caldwell of the Oakland (California) Police Department's Bureau of Identification. Its original membership roster consisted of 22 men. Today, the association has more than 7,000 male and female members in the United States and throughout the world.

Crime scene investigators have come a long way since the early days of criminal investigation. Today, they use sophisticated equipment and scientific procedures to gather and analyze evidence. This career has been made exceedingly popular by the television show *CSI*. Although work as a crime scene investigator may not be as glamorous and exciting as depicted on television and in movies, this field offers a great opportunity to make a difference in the world and help forensic scientists solve crimes.

THE JOB

At the scene of an actual or suspected crime, the first thing a crime scene investigator must do is secure the scene (if it hasn't been secured already by a police officer) using barricades, tape, or the assistance of police officers. Then they collect and label evidence. This pains-taking task may involve searching for spent bullets or bits of an exploded bomb and other objects scattered by an explosion. They might look for footprints, fingerprints, and tire tracks that must be recorded or preserved by plaster casting before they are wiped out. They collect blood samples, body fluids, hairs, and other evidence.

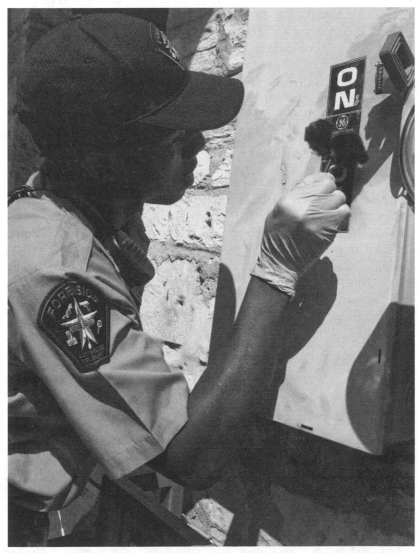

A crime scene investigator dusts for fingerprints at a crime scene. *(Marjorie Kamys Cotera, Daemmrich Photography, The Image Works)*

Since crime scenes must eventually be cleaned up, crime scene investigators take notes and photographs to preserve the arrangement of objects, bodies, and debris. They diagram the scene of the crime by making a floor plan or map that shows the exact location of bodies, weapons, and furniture. They refer to this plan when working on the case. Crime scene investigators also interview victims and witnesses to gather more information about the case.

When traveling to the scene of a crime, crime scene investigators may have to carry cases of tools, cameras, and chemicals. In order not to risk contaminating evidence, they must follow strict procedures for collecting and testing evidence; these procedures can be extremely time-consuming and thus require a great deal of patience. Forensic experts also need to be able to arrive at and present their findings impartially. At large law enforcement agencies, they often work as part of a team under the direction of a senior investigator.

In very large agencies, crime scene investigators may have very specialized duties—that often involve considerable time in medical laboratories or morgues. One investigator may work only with cadavers in a morgue, another may work only in a lab analyzing evidence, another may investigate and photograph crime scenes, and another may analyze fingerprints. Some investigators assist criminalists, and use instruments of science and engineering to examine physical evidence. They use spectroscopes, microscopes, gas chromatographs, infrared and ultraviolet light, microphotography, and other lab measuring and testing equipment to analyze fibers, fabric, dust, soils, paint chips, glass fragments, fire accelerants, paper and ink, and other substances in order to identify their composition and origin. They analyze poisons, drugs, and other substances found in bodies by examining tissue samples, stomach contents, and blood samples. They analyze and classify blood, blood alcohol, semen, hair, fingernails, teeth, human and animal bones and tissue, and other biological specimens. Using samples of the genetic material DNA, they can match a person with a sample of body tissue. They also examine the physical properties of firearms, bullets, and explosives.

REQUIREMENTS
High School
In high school, you can begin to prepare for this field by taking a heavy concentration of science courses, including chemistry, biology, physiology, and physics. Computer skills are also important. A basic grounding in spoken and written communications will be useful because crime scene investigators must write very detailed reports and are sometimes called on to present their findings in court.

Postsecondary Training

Some smaller agencies require investigators to only have a high school diploma. Most larger agencies require applicants to have at least some postsecondary training. Many investigators have a minimum of an associate's degree in forensic science, one of the physical sciences (especially biology or chemistry), or a closely related field. Forensic science courses and programs are offered by many community and four-year colleges. Courses may include training in crime scene photography, fingerprint processing, blood splatter analysis, criminal profiling, and forensic biology. Visit the Web sites of the American Academy of Forensic Sciences (http://www.aafs.org) and the Council on Forensic Science Education (http://www.criminology.fsu.edu/COFSE/default. html) for lists of colleges and universities that offer classes and programs in forensic science.

After they are hired, crime scene investigators receive on-the-job training. They learn how to process crime scenes, take photographs, and document their findings, among other skills. This experience may be informal or may be provided through a formal internship or apprenticeship.

Certification or Licensing

The International Association for Identification offers the voluntary crime scene certification. The certification consists of a tri-level program: Level I: certified crime scene investigator, Level II: certified crime scene analyst, and Level III: certified senior crime scene analyst. To attain the first level, applicants must have at least one year of experience in the field, have completed at least 48 hours of approved instruction in crime scene-related courses within the past five years, and pass a written test. Applicants for the upper levels must meet more stringent experience and educational requirements. Certification is also available in several other categories including bloodstain pattern examiner, footwear, forensic art, forensic photography, latent print certification, and tenprint fingerprint.

Other Requirements

When gathering evidence and analyzing it, crime scene investigators need to be able to concentrate, sometimes in crowded, noisy situations. For this reason, they must be adaptable and able to work in a variety of environments, including dangerous or unpleasant places.

Many crime scenes are grisly and may be extremely distressing for beginning workers and even for more seasoned professionals. In addition, crime scene investigators will regularly view corpses, and more often than not these corpses will have been mutilated in some way or be in varying degrees of decomposition. Individuals interested in this field need to develop the detachment and objectivity necessary to view corpses and extract specimens for testing and analysis.

In addition to these skills, crime scene investigators should be able to work as a member of a team, be organized, have excellent communication skills, be able to multitask, be highly ethical, be able to follow instructions, and be detail oriented.

EXPLORING

A large community police department may have a crime lab of its own whose investigators can give you specific information about their work and the preparation that helped them build their careers. Smaller communities often use the lab facilities of a larger city nearby or the state police. A school counselor or a representative of the local police may be able to help you arrange a tour of these labs. Lectures in forensic science given at universities or police conventions may also be open to students. Web sites devoted to forensic science can provide good sources of information on educational requirements and the daily and professional experiences of people crime scene investigators. One such site is CSI Web Adventures (http://forensics.rice.edu).

EMPLOYERS

Approximately 13,000 crime scene investigators are employed in the United States. Crime scene investigators typically work for large police departments or state or law enforcement agencies nationwide. They may also work in the private sector in large corporations or small firms. They may be employed by the military, medical examiner's offices, state's attorney offices, and law firms. Many civilian crime scene investigators work part time.

STARTING OUT

Contact large police departments or state or law enforcement agencies in your area to inquire about job opportunities. Many professional organizations, such as the International Crime Scene Investigators Association (http://www.icsia.org), post openings on their Web sites.

ADVANCEMENT

If sworn police officers, investigators may move up through the ranks. In a large crime laboratory, investigators usually advance from an assistant's position to working independently at one or more special types of analysis. From there they may advance to a position as project leader or being in charge of all aspects of one particular investigation. In smaller labs, one investigator may have to fill many roles. With experience, such an investigator may progress to more responsible work but receive no advancement in title.

Advancement opportunities for civilian investigators are more limited. They may advance to the position of crime scene supervisor or make lateral moves to larger agencies that offer higher salaries and/or opportunities for advancement.

EARNINGS

Earnings for crime scene investigators vary by employer, geographic location, and educational and skill levels. The U.S. Department of Labor reports that the median salary for forensic science technicians was $49,860 in 2008. Salaries ranged from less than $30,990 to $80,330 or more. Forensic science technicians employed by local government agencies earned mean annual salaries of $53,300, and those employed by state agencies earned $51,910.

Full-time investigators in law enforcement can expect to be provided with health, hospital, disability, and life insurance benefits.

WORK ENVIRONMENT

If you get queasy around the sight of blood or other bodily fluids, this is not the job for you. Crime scene investigators spend much of their time working at crime scenes that feature victims of violent crime who have been shot, stabbed, strangled, poisoned, or otherwise killed. This work can be physically demanding. Investigators must often kneel, stoop, or climb to gather evidence. They may have to work outdoors in extremely hot or cold conditions or otherwise challenging settings. Investigators are sometimes exposed to chemicals or other hazards; in these instances, they must wear protective equipment such as respirators. Crime scene investigators work a variety of shifts, including nights and weekends.

OUTLOOK

Employment for crime scene investigators is expected to grow much faster than the average for all occupations through 2016, according to the U.S. Department of Labor. Population increases, a rising crime rate, and the greater emphasis on scientific methodology in crime investigation have increased the need for trained investigators.

Crime scene investigators who are employed by state and local public safety departments should experience especially strong employment opportunities, although some government agencies may be under pressure to reduce staff because of budget problems. Crime scene investigators with four-year degrees in forensic science will enjoy the best employment prospects.

FOR MORE INFORMATION

For information on careers and colleges and universities that offer forensic science programs, contact
   American Academy of Forensic Sciences
   410 North 21st Street
   Colorado Springs, CO 80904-2712
   Tel: 719-636-1100
   http://www.aafs.org

For information on crime scene reconstruction, contact
   Association for Crime Scene Reconstruction
   http://www.acsr.org

For information on colleges and universities that offer forensic science programs, contact
   The Council on Forensic Science Education
   http://www.criminology.fsu.edu/COFSE/default.html

To learn more about forensic services at the FBI, visit the FBI Laboratory Division's Web site.
   Federal Bureau of Investigation (FBI)
   J. Edgar Hoover Building
   935 Pennsylvania Avenue, NW
   Washington, DC 20535-0001
   Tel: 202-324-3000
   http://www.fbi.gov/hq/lab/labhome.htm

For information on career paths, contact
   Forensic Sciences Foundation
   410 North 21st Street
   Colorado Springs, CO 80904-2712
   Tel: 719-636-1100
   http://www.forensicsciencesfoundation.org/career_paths/
      careers.htm

For information on certification, contact
International Association for Identification
2535 Pilot Knob Road, Suite 117
Mendota Heights, MN 55120-1120
Tel: 651-681-8566
http://www.theiai.org

For career information, contact
International Crime Scene Investigators Association
Email: info@icsia.org
http://www.icsia.org

Criminalists

QUICK FACTS

School Subjects
Biology
Chemistry

Personal Skills
Following instructions
Technical/scientific

Work Environment
Primarily indoors
Primarily multiple locations

Minimum Education Level
Bachelor's degree

Salary Range
$25,000 to $40,000 to
$100,000+

Certification or Licensing
Recommended

Outlook
About as fast as the average

DOT
029

GOE
N/A

NOC
N/A

O*NET-SOC
N/A

OVERVIEW

Criminalists are forensic scientists who apply scientific principles and methods to the analysis, identification, and classification of physical evidence relating to criminal (or suspected criminal) cases. They do much of their work in laboratories, where they subject evidence to tests and then record the results. Criminalists may also be called upon to testify as expert witnesses and to present scientific findings in court.

HISTORY

Basic forensic science concepts (such as fingerprint analysis and the collection of physical evidence) have been used to solve crimes for thousands of years. But it was not until the last 120 years or so that forensic science developed as a scientific discipline.

In the late 19th century scientists learned to analyze and classify poisons so their presence could be traced in a body. At about the same time, a controversy arose over the different methods being used to identify individuals positively. Fingerprinting emerged in the early 20th century as the most reliable method of personal identification. With the advent of X-ray technology, experts could rely on dental records to substitute for fingerprint analysis when a corpse was in advanced stages of decomposition and the condition of the skin had deteriorated.

Forensic pathology (medical examination of suspicious or unexplained deaths) also came into prominence at this time, as did ballistics, which is the study of projectiles and how they are shot from firearms. The study of ballistics was aided by the invention of the comparison microscope, which enabled an investigator to look at bullets side by side and compare their individual markings. Since individual gun barrels "scar" bullets in a unique pattern, similar markings found on different bullets may prove that they were fired from the same weapon.

These investigations by pioneer forensic scientists led the courts and the police to acknowledge the value of scientifically examined physical evidence in establishing guilt or innocence, confirming identity, proving authenticity of documents, and establishing cause of death. As the result of this acceptance by the legal and law enforcement communities, crime laboratories were established. One of the first, largest, and most complete laboratories is that of the Federal Bureau of Investigation (FBI), founded in 1932. Today, the FBI Laboratory examines many thousands of pieces of evidence each year, and its employees present their findings in trials all over the United States and around the world. As the forensic sciences proved their worth, crime laboratories were established in larger cities and by state police departments. These laboratories are used in turn by many communities too small to support labs of their own. The scientific analysis of evidence has become a key part of police procedure, and new forensic advances, such as DNA testing, are being developed every day.

THE JOB

Criminalists use scientific instruments to examine many different types of physical evidence from crime scenes. They use spectroscopes, microscopes, gas chromatographs, infrared and ultraviolet light, microphotography, and other lab measuring and testing equipment to analyze such items as fibers, fabric, dust, soils, paint chips, glass fragments, fire accelerants, paper and ink, and other substances in order to identify their composition and origin. For example, criminalists might analyze flecks of paint found embedded in a hit-and-run accident victim and paint samples from a vehicle suspected of being used in the accident and either confirm or rule out that they match. Criminalists also analyze biological evidence such as blood, semen, hair, fingernails, teeth, human and animal bones and tissue, and other biological specimens. Using samples of the genetic material DNA, they can identify a person with a sample of body tissue. Criminalists can discover and analyze poisons, drugs, and other substances found in bodies by examining tissue samples, stomach contents, and blood samples. For example, by studying the content of a murder victim's stomach, they can determine when and what the victim last ate, which can be useful to investigators in creating a timeline leading up the murder. Or they might discover traces of poison in a person's blood or body tissue that can explain a baffling illness or death.

Criminalists study documents to determine whether they are forged or genuine. They also examine the physical properties of firearms, bullets, and explosives. By examining the bullets fired into the victim of a crime or left at a crime scene, criminalists can determine what type of gun fired the bullets. In addition, they can usually note microscopic characteristics of the bullet that can be matched to the gun that fired that bullet, should it be found. Criminalists also work with impressions, such as those of tire markings or footprints left at the scene of a crime. They can often identify the brand and type of tire and what vehicles they are typically found on; or the size, type, and sometimes even the exact brand of shoe that left an imprint. All are potentially useful bits of information for law enforcement officials involved in a criminal investigation.

Criminalists spend the bulk of their time in the laboratory working with physical evidence collected from crime scenes. In addition to the actual testing and analysis of evidence, they must provide detailed written documentation of everything they do, and they must also take care to properly catalogue and store evidence throughout the process. Their documentation often includes photographs, illustrations, or video. When they are done, they compile their documentation and findings into a report. Criminalists seldom have direct contact with persons involved in actual or suspected crimes or with police investigators except when they themselves might be involved in collecting evidence, and when they report their findings.

Criminalists typically do not interpret their findings relative to the criminal investigation in which they are involved; that is the work of police investigators. The purpose of crime lab work is to provide reliable scientific analysis of evidence that can then be used in criminal investigations and, if needed later, in court proceedings. Criminalists may be asked to testify in legal proceedings regarding the contents of their reports.

REQUIREMENTS

High School

You will need at least a bachelor's degree to work as a criminalist. In high school, take as many science courses as possible, including chemistry, biology, physiology, and physics. Mathematics and computer courses will also be very useful. Take English and speech classes to help you develop your communication skills. These skills will help you write detailed reports and present your findings in court.

Postsecondary Training

You will need at least a bachelor's degree in forensic science, chemistry, biology, molecular biology, physics, criminalistics, or a related field to work as a criminalist. Many criminalists in top positions have graduate degrees. Visit the Web sites of the American Academy of Forensic Sciences (http://www.aafs.org) and the Council on Forensic Science Education (http://www.criminology.fsu.edu/COFSE/default.html) for lists of colleges and universities that offer classes and programs in forensic science and related fields.

Once hired, criminalists participate in on-the-job training that can last from a few months to a few years. They are expected to take continuing education classes, seminars, and workshops throughout their careers in order to keep their skills on par with changing technology and investigative techniques.

Certification or Licensing

Voluntary certification is available from the American Board of Criminalistics. Certification is available in comprehensive criminalistics, as well as in drug analysis, fire debris analysis, molecular biology, trace evidence-hairs and fibers, and trace evidence-paints and polymers. Applicants must satisfy education and experience requirements and take and pass an examination. Certification is valid for five years, at which point individuals can become recertified by completing additional training or casework, or by taking the examination again. The American College of Forensic Examiners, International Association for Identification, and the Association of Firearm and Tool Mark Examiners also offer certification in a variety of categories. Contact these organizations for more information.

Other Requirements

To be successful in this field, you should have an aptitude for scientific investigation, an inquiring and logical mind, and the ability to make precise measurements and observations. Patience and persistence are important qualities, as is a good memory. Criminalists must constantly bear in mind that the accuracy of their lab investigations can have great consequences for others. You also must be highly ethical when preparing reports and testifying in court. You should never let any personal biases cloud your investigative work. Criminalists also need good communication skills in order to interact successfully with coworkers, write detailed reports, and provide testimony in court that can be easily understood by jury members, lawyers, and judges.

EXPLORING

Read as many books as you can about forensic science and criminalistics. Here are a few suggestions: *Forensic Science: Fundamentals and Investigations,* by Anthony J. Bertino; *Forensic Science for High School Students,* by John Funkhouser; and *Criminalistics: An Introduction to Forensic Science,* 9th ed., by Richard Saferstein. You can also visit the Web sites of professional associations to learn more about careers in criminalistics. The American Academy of Forensic Sciences offers an overview of the career of criminalist at its Web site (http://www.aafs.org). Another option is to ask your high school science teacher or career counselor to help arrange a tour of a crime lab or a presentation by a criminalist.

EMPLOYERS

Criminalists typically work for large police departments, state law enforcement agencies, district attorney's offices, medical examiner's offices, and colleges and universities. They may also be employed by the federal government (including the FBI, the military, Drug Enforcement Administration, United States Postal Service, Secret Service, Central Intelligence Agency, U.S. Fish and Wildlife Service, and the Bureau of Alcohol, Tobacco, Firearms, and Explosives).

STARTING OUT

Crime labs are maintained by the federal government and by state and local governments. Applications should be made directly to the personnel department of the government agency supporting the lab. Civil service appointments usually require applicants to take an examination. Such appointments are usually widely advertised well in advance of the application date. Those working for the FBI or other law enforcement agencies usually undergo background checks, which examine their character, background, previous employers, and family and friends.

ADVANCEMENT

In a large crime laboratory, criminalists usually advance from an entry-level position to working independently at one or more special types of analysis. From there they may advance to a position as project leader or supervising all aspects of one particular investigation. In smaller labs, one criminalist may have to fill many roles. With experience, such a criminalist may progress to more responsible work but receive no advancement in title. They may also become laboratory directors, become technical specialists in a particular field (such as ballistics), or work as high school and college educators. Criminalists who work for police departments may pursue advancement with a different local or state government agency or apply for positions with the FBI.

Crucial to advancement is further education. Criminalists need to be familiar with scientific procedures such as gas chromatography, ultraviolet and infrared spectrophotometry, mass spectroscopy, electrophoresis, polarizing microscopy, light microscopy, and conventional and isoelectric focusing; knowledge of these analytical techniques and procedures is taught or more fully explored at the master's and doctorate levels. Other, more specific areas of forensics, such as DNA analysis, require advanced degrees in molecular biology and genetics.

EARNINGS

Salaries for criminalists vary based on geographic location, employer, and educational and skill levels. Little information is available regarding salaries for criminalists. Based on an analysis of job postings for criminalists throughout the United States, it is estimated that criminalists earn starting salaries that range from $25,000 to $40,000. Experienced workers earn anywhere from $40,000 to more than $100,000.

Benefits for full-time workers include vacation and sick time, health insurance, and pension or 401(k) plans.

WORK ENVIRONMENT

Criminalists usually perform the analysis portion of their work in clean, quiet, air-conditioned laboratories. In large labs, criminalists often work as part of a team under the direction of a senior criminalist. They may experience eyestrain and contact with strong chemicals, but little heavy physical work is involved. Some criminalists must be on-call 24 hours a day—ready to report to work at a moment's notice. This scheduling can sometimes create stress in a criminalist's personal life.

OUTLOOK

Employment of criminalists should be good during the next decade. There is currently a backlog of cases at many crime laboratories, and criminalists will be needed to work on these and new cases.

Opportunities will vary by geographic region. Opportunities will be best in states that provide strong funding for their forensic science laboratories, and weaker in those that do not. Criminalists with advanced degrees and certification will have the best job prospects.

FOR MORE INFORMATION

For information on forensic careers, education, and its membership section for criminalists, contact
    American Academy of Forensic Sciences
    410 North 21st Street
    Colorado Springs, CO 80904-2712
    Tel: 719-636-1100
    http://www.aafs.org

For information on certification, contact
    American Board of Criminalistics
    PO Box 1123
    Wausau, WI 54402-1123
    http://www.criminalistics.com

For information on forensic science and certification, contact
    American College of Forensic Examiners
    2750 East Sunshine Street
    Springfield, MO 65804-2047
    Tel: 800-423-9737
    http://www.acfei.com

For information on careers and publications, contact
    American Society of Questioned Document Examiners
    http://www.asqde.org

For information on certification, contact
    Association of Firearm and Tool Mark Examiners
    http://www.afte.org

For useful forensic science Web links, visit the association's Web site.
    Association of Forensic DNA Analysts and Administrators
    PO Box 4983
    Austin, TX 78765-4983
    http://www.afdaa.org

For information on colleges and universities that offer forensic science programs, contact
Council on Forensic Science Education
http://www.criminology.fsu.edu/COFSE/default.html

To learn more about forensic services at the FBI, visit the FBI Laboratory Division's Web site.
Federal Bureau of Investigation (FBI)
J. Edgar Hoover Building
935 Pennsylvania Avenue, NW
Washington, DC 20535-0001
Tel: 202-324-3000
http://www.fbi.gov and http://www.fbi.gov/hq/lab/labhome.htm

For information on career paths, contact
Forensic Sciences Foundation
410 North 21st Street
Colorado Springs, CO 80904-2712
Tel: 719-636-1100
http://www.forensicsciencesfoundation.org/career_paths/
   careers.htm

For information on certification, contact
International Association for Identification
2535 Pilot Knob Road, Suite 117
Mendota Heights, MN 55120-1120
Tel: 651-681-8566
http://www.theiai.org

For information on bloodstain pattern analysis, contact
International Association of Bloodstain Pattern Analysts
http://www.iabpa.org

———————————— **INTERVIEW** ————————————

Wayne Moorehead is a senior forensic scientist. He has worked in the field of criminalistics for more than 32 years. Wayne discussed his career with the editors of Careers in Focus: Forensics.

Q. What made you want to enter this field?
A. A combination of several life events led me to my career. Since I was in first grade I had an interest in science. When I was 10

years old, in the manuals of the microscope set and the chemistry set I had were experiments that integrated science with applications to law enforcement. During the summer of my junior year in high school I began to read parts of a book on criminalistics by Paul Kirk, *Crime Investigation*. I entered the University of California (UC) at Berkeley as a chemistry major, but after my first criminalistics class during my second year and a suggestion by the professor, I changed majors. While still in college I worked for the UC police department in the capacity of an evidence technician, or what is known now as a forensic specialist. I knew I wanted to pursue criminalistics for a career.

Q. What are your main and secondary job duties?

A. The main job of a forensic scientist, or criminalist, is to provide answers about evidence by solving analytical questions in legal matters. These questions may come from the forensic scientist, the investigator, the district attorney, or another legally significant party (coroner's office, forensic pathologist, judge, etc.). The secondary job is to interpret the results of the analysis in the context of the case based on the information supplied or known while trying to inhibit either the prosecutor or the defense attorneys from misrepresenting the meaning of the results. Unlike the attorneys, the forensic scientist is the only advocate for the evidence.

Q. What are some of the pros and cons of being a forensic scientist?

A. With a bachelor of science or a bachelor of art degree (BS/BA) the forensic scientist is solely responsible for his or her work. In other scientific areas, the person with the BS/BA does not have the authority and responsibility like that found in forensic science, including routine court testimony. The work is often analytically or intellectually challenging while helping society and the legal system.

The cons are that there are pressures to produce high-quality analyses in each case while completing a large number of cases in a given time period. Not only do your peers review your work, but others may review it, including your supervisor, the quality assurance section, the management, the prosecuting/plaintiff and defense attorneys, and the forensic expert for the defense. Occasionally, court testimony can be very demanding or stressful regardless of who is asking the questions.

Q. What are the most important personal and professional qualities for forensic scientists?

A. The forensic scientist must have character, honesty, and integrity. As with every science, having an insatiable curiosity is very important as well as learning to make observations and to document them. Fact memorization is less important than knowing where to find the information needed and being able to properly apply knowledge to analytical problem solving. The forensic scientist may have to call on every part of his or her knowledge and experience to answer questions about the crime scene and evidence. Forensic scientists are not interested in the outcome of a trial (e.g., whether the jury found the defendant guilty or innocent); they worry whether the jury believed their testimony and found them credible.

Q. What is the future employment outlook for forensic scientists?

A. With the economy declining, the immediate outlook is fairly bleak with not many agencies hiring. As a result of the National Academy of Sciences report on forensic science and the number of experienced scientists retiring, there will be many future opportunities in forensic science for the prepared candidate. A written test and at least one oral interview are part of the pathway to employment. Attending regional and national forensic science meetings, reading journals and textbooks, taking classes, and developing interests in related forensic science areas prepare the candidate for a successful interview.

Q. What advice would you give to high school students who want to enter this field?

A. Focus on science classes in high school and in college major in a natural or applied science. Science majors include, but are not limited to chemistry, biology, biochemistry, zoology, geology, molecular biology, medical technologist, etc. You *must* have a minimum of two years of chemistry (general chemistry and organic chemistry) although more chemistry is recommended such as a quantitative analysis class. If you are interested in DNA analysis, then classes on molecular biology, genetics, biochemistry, and statistics are recommended. Take a variety of scientific classes to broaden your knowledge. Geology, physiology, and botany are examples.

A thorough background investigation will be conducted in order to be hired so stay away from drugs and avoid people who take, possess, or sell illegal substances. Drive so that you don't acquire tickets, keep your credit clean, and don't commit a crime.

Fingerprint Analysts

OVERVIEW

Fingerprint analysts work with fingerprint evidence. They obtain and classify the fingerprints of people, such as those who are arrested, as well as process evidence recovered from crime scenes to find and develop fingerprints that can be used to identify suspects or victims.

HISTORY

Although modern day use of fingerprints for identification purposes has only developed in the last couple of centuries, fingerprints and their characteristics have been noted long before that.

Some paintings and rock art of prehistoric people show crude reproductions of finger and hand prints, and the Babylonians in 500 B.C. included fingerprints on clay tablets that recorded business transactions; the Chinese were also using fingerprints in a similar manner. But the study of fingerprints, their unique characteristics, and their use for positively identifying people didn't develop until more modern times. In 1686 an Italian anatomy professor by the name of Marcello Malpighi was credited with noting different characteristics of fingerprints, such as ridges and loops. In 1823 Jan Purkinje, a Czechoslovakian anatomy professor, published a paper on fingerprints. He identified nine primary types of fingerprints and proposed a classification system.

The uniqueness of fingerprints and their ability to be used as a method of identification that would be permanent and unique to each individual was raised in 1880 by Henry Faulds, a Scottish physician, and William James Herschel, a British officer working in India who for years had included finger and palm prints on documentation,

QUICK FACTS

School Subjects
Biology
Mathematics

Personal Skills
Technical/scientific

Work Environment
Indoors and outdoors
One location with some
    travel

Minimum Education Level
High school diploma

Salary Range
$30,990 to $49,860 to
    $80,330+

Certification or Licensing
Voluntary

Outlook
About as fast as the average

DOT
188, 375

GOE
04.03.02

NOC
N/A

O*NET-SOC
19-4092.00

primarily when dealing with illiterate people. Their work was expanded on by the English scientist, Sir Francis Galton. Galton proposed what is generally recognized as the first system for fingerprint classification that used patterns of whorls, arches, and loops, and published his comprehensive findings in *Fingerprints* (1892). Around the same time, an Argentinean police employee named Juan Vucetich created a different fingerprint classification system that is still used in many Latin and South American countries today.

In the United States, the first use of fingerprints as means of identification began in New York in the early 1900s. Initially fingerprints were used by the state's Civil Service Commission, but in 1903 the state's prison system adopted their use as well. Branches of law enforcement and corrections in other cities, states, and the federal government followed suit. As the use of fingerprints as a means of criminal identification became more widespread, the Federal Bureau of Investigation (FBI) established an Identification Division, and in 1924, the new division created a central collection of more than 800,000 sets of fingerprints. More than 100 million sets of fingerprint were processed by the FBI by 1946, and by 1971, that number had surpassed more than 200 million.

With advances in technology came advances in how fingerprints were stored and retrieved. In 1977 the FBI's Automated Fingerprint Identification System (AFIS) database first began using computerized scans of fingerprints, and in 1996, computerized searches of the AFIS database were possible. Further upgrades and capabilities were introduced in 1999 when the FBI introduced the Integrated Automated Fingerprint Identification System, facilitating the vital role that fingerprints can play in crime solving in the 21st century.

THE JOB

Fingerprint analysts collect, catalog, and compare fingerprints of suspected criminals with records to determine if the people who left the fingerprints at the scene of a crime were involved in previous crimes. They may also try to match the fingerprints of unknown corpses with fingerprint records to establish their identity. Fingerprints and impressions left by the palms of the hand and soles and toes of the feet that have been left on an object or surface and collected from the surface or object are known as latent prints. They are usually invisible to the human eye and must be processed to make them visible. Fingerprints purposely obtained from a person, such as someone who has been arrested, are known as ten-prints (meaning prints from all 10 fingers).

Sometimes fingerprints are readily visible and easy to collect from crime scenes or evidence, such as those left by a finger covered in blood or another substance, or those that are left in matter that easily retains the imprint of the finger, such as a layer of dust or an object made of a soft substance. Retrieving fingerprints can sometimes be as easy and straightforward as lifting them off a surface with a flexible tape, which can be brought back to the laboratory for further evaluation and matching. Oftentimes, though, the discovery and retrieval of fingerprints may be difficult and require specialized processes. Some fingerprints might not even be visible without extra intervention, such as the use of lasers or other light sources shined on a surface. Other methods involve dusting glassware, windows, or walls with a fine powder or spraying chemicals on a surface. The powders and chemical sprays contrast with many different surfaces and will highlight any fingerprints that remain so they can be collected and/or photographed. Even fingerprints that have been collected by other methods are usually photographed as well; this makes it easier to store and input fingerprints into record-keeping systems.

Once fingerprints have been obtained from a crime scene or a piece of evidence, fingerprint analysts might compare these new

A fingerprint analyst for Interpol pores over fingerprints taken from the bodies of unidentified Asian tsunami victims. *(Daniel Lovering, AP Photo)*

prints against those found after the commission of similar crimes. A fingerprint analyst may keep individual files on current crimes and note any similarities between them. The fingerprint analyst documents this information and transfers it and the fingerprints to the main record-keeping system, often a large computer database system known as the Automated Fingerprint Identification System. In the last decade or so, computers have greatly enhanced the possibility of matching new fingerprints to those already on file, and AFIS and similar databases can be used to scan and compare a large number of fingerprints in a fraction of the time it would take a fingerprint analyst to manually compare just a few sets of fingerprints. The Integrated Automated Fingerprint Identification System, maintained by the Federal Bureau of Investigation, is the largest such database in the world. In addition, many levels of law enforcement maintain their own local AFIS.

Fingerprint analysts typically work in offices and laboratories, although they also travel to crime scenes to collect evidence and to courthouses to testify regarding evidence.

Although most fingerprint analysts are civilian workers, some are sworn law enforcement officers.

REQUIREMENTS

High School

General high school classes that will help prepare you for a career as a fingerprint analyst include biology, chemistry, English, speech, and mathematics. You should also take computer science courses since you will use computers to do much of your work. Be sure to take any classes in forensic science or criminal justice that are available.

Postsecondary Training

You will need at least a high school diploma to land a job as a fingerprint analyst. It is highly recommended, though, that you earn at least an associate's degree in fingerprint classification, forensic science, or a related area in order to obtain employment at large law enforcement agencies. The American Academy of Forensic Sciences offers a list of colleges and universities that offer degrees in fingerprint classification and related fields at its Web site (http://www.aafs.org).

Once hired, fingerprint analysts receive on-the-job training that includes classroom work and hands-on experience that is supervised by a senior fingerprint analyst. To stay up to date with changing technology and investigative techniques, fingerprint analysts continue to learn throughout their careers by participating in educational conferences, workshops, and seminars.

Certification or Licensing
The International Association for Identification offers two voluntary certifications for fingerprint analysts: latent print certification and tenprint fingerprint certification. Contact the association for more information.

The American College of Forensic Examiners offers the certified forensic consultant program, which provides an overview of the U.S. judicial system. This certification would be useful for fingerprint analysts who are required to testify in court. Contact the college for more information.

Other Requirements
A successful fingerprint analyst must have good organizational skills; be able to work as a member of a team, as well as work without supervision when necessary; and have good communication skills in order to document his or her findings, interact successfully with coworkers, and provide effective testimony during court proceedings. Fingerprint analysts also need to have excellent vision in order to properly analyze fingerprints. Other important skills include punctuality, the ability to follow instructions, good observational skills, and the ability to meet deadlines.

EXPLORING

There are many ways to learn about the study of fingerprints and the work of fingerprint analysts. You can read books about the field such as *Fingerprints: Analysis and Understanding,* by Mark R. Hawthorne; *Handbook of Fingerprint Recognition,* 2nd ed., by Davide Maltoni, Dario Maio, Anil K. Jain, and Salil Prabhakar; and *Automated Fingerprint Identification Systems,* by Peter Komarinski. You can learn fingerprint lingo by visiting http://www. fprints.nwlean.net, which offers definitions of more than 900 commonly used terms in the field. Other interesting Web sites include Ridges and Furrows (http://ridgesandfurrows.homestead.com), FBI: All About Fingerprints (http://www.fbi.gov/hq/cjisd/cjis.htm), and The History of Fingerprints (http://onin.com/fp/fphistory.html). Ask your high school science teacher or counselor to arrange an information interview with a fingerprint analyst. Maybe they could even arrange a tour of a crime lab, where you can watch fingerprint analysts at work.

EMPLOYERS

Fingerprint analysts are employed by local, state, and federal law enforcement agencies. They also work as educators at the college level.

STARTING OUT

Law enforcement agencies typically hire fingerprint analysts who have some experience working with fingerprints. This experience is often gained during one's college education, including participation in an internship. Applicants should contact law enforcement agencies directly for information on job openings. Many of these organizations have Web sites that detail available jobs and application requirements.

ADVANCEMENT

Fingerprint analysts advance by being assigned supervisory duties, earning higher pay, or working for larger organizations. Others pursue additional training to become police officers, crime scene investigators, criminalists, or forensic scientists (such as forensic chemists or forensic biologists). Others become teachers at the high school or college levels. Police officers who work as fingerprint analysts advance by gaining rank, such as becoming detectives, sergeants, captains, and so on.

WORK ENVIRONMENT

Fingerprint analysts generally perform their work in laboratories and offices. They may also travel to other areas, such as crime scenes. They may be called to testify in legal proceedings to explain their analysis of fingerprints in a specific case, or to simply explain fingerprint identification and collection procedures in general. Fingerprint analysts work a standard 40-hour week, but have shifts that may require them to be on duty at all hours, including on weekends.

EARNINGS

There is no comprehensive salary information available for fingerprint analysts, but the U.S. Department of Labor (DoL) provides information on earnings for forensic science technicians (a category that includes technicians who specialize in fingerprint analysis). The DoL reports that the median salary for forensic science technicians was $49,860 in 2008. Salaries ranged from less than $30,990 to $80,330 or more. Forensic science technicians employed by local government agencies earned mean annual salaries of $53,300, and those employed by state agencies earned $51,910. Earnings for fingerprint analysts vary by employer, geographic location, and educational and skill levels.

Salaried fingerprint analysts usually receive benefits such as vacation days, sick leave, health and life insurance, and a savings and pension program. Self-employed fingerprint analysts must provide their own benefits.

OUTLOOK

The U.S. Department of Labor predicts that employment for forensic science technicians (a category that includes technicians who specialize in fingerprint analysis) is expected to grow much faster than the average for all occupations through 2016. Despite this prediction, employment for fingerprint analysts is not expected to be as good as a result of strong competition for jobs and advances in technology that have allowed fewer analysts to study more prints. Fingerprint analysts with advanced education and considerable experience in the field will have the best employment prospects.

FOR MORE INFORMATION

For information on forensic careers and education, contact
American Academy of Forensic Sciences
410 North 21st Street
Colorado Springs, CO 80904-2712
Tel: 719-636-1100
http://www.aafs.org

For information on forensic science and certification, contact
American College of Forensic Examiners
2750 East Sunshine Street
Springfield, MO 65804-2047
Tel: 800-423-9737
http://www.acfei.com

To learn more about forensic services at the FBI, visit the FBI Laboratory Division's Web site.
Federal Bureau of Investigation (FBI)
J. Edgar Hoover Building
935 Pennsylvania Avenue, NW

Washington, DC 20535-0001
Tel: 202-324-3000
http://www.fbi.gov/hq/lab/labhome.htm

For information on certification, contact
International Association for Identification
2535 Pilot Knob Road, Suite 117
Mendota Heights, MN 55120-1120
Tel: 651-681-8566
http://www.theiai.org

Fire Investigators

OVERVIEW

Fire investigators analyze the cause, origin, and circumstances of fires involving loss of life and considerable property damage; interrogate witnesses and prepare investigation reports; and arrest and seek prosecution of arsonists. They are also known as *fire marshals*. Approximately 13,000 fire investigators and inspectors (who perform examinations to enforce fire-prevention laws, ordinances, and codes, among other tasks) are employed in the United States.

HISTORY

The origins of fires have been investigated, at least informally, ever since the first suspicious fire caused the loss of property or injury or death to humans. Early fire investigators were typically firefighters who used their knowledge of how accidental fires started and burned to identify those that had suspicious origins. It was not until the development of modern analytical techniques and equipment that the work of fire investigation became a formal career. Today, fire investigators play a key role in determining the cause of suspicious fires and stopping arson, which is the second leading cause of death in the United States and the leading cause of property damage due to fires.

THE JOB

Fire investigators look for evidence pointing to the causes of fires, accidental or criminal. Once fires are extinguished, especially if they

QUICK FACTS

School Subjects
Biology
Chemistry

Personal Skills
Leadership/management
Technical/scientific

Work Environment
Indoors and outdoors
Primarily multiple locations

Minimum Education Level
Some postsecondary training

Salary Range
$32,680 to $53,030 to
$100,000+

Certification or Licensing
Recommended (certification)
Required by certain states
(licensing)

Outlook
About as fast as the average

DOT
373

GOE
04.03.01

NOC
N/A

O*NET-SOC
33-2021.00

Did You Know?

- It is difficult to catch arsonists. Arrests are made in only one in 20 of intentionally set fires.
- The number of arsons committed in the United States has been decreasing since 1985.
- More than 50 percent of arsonists are under the age of 18.

Source: National Fire Protection Association

are of suspicious origin or cause death or injury, investigators look for evidence of arson; that is, fires that are deliberately set to obtain insurance money or for other reasons, such as anger, vandalism, or to cover-up evidence of another crime (such as a murder). Fire investigators determine whether the fire was incendiary (arson) or accidental, and then try to figure out what caused it. This information is very important to the fire-protection community. In cases of arson it is the fire investigator's responsibility to collect information or evidence that can be used to prosecute the fire starter. For example, the fire investigator must determine what fuel, or accelerant, (gasoline, paper, etc.) was used to start the fire and in the process may discover devices that were also used. Fire investigators may submit reports to a district attorney, or arrest suspected arsonists (if they have police authority). Fire investigators also gather information from accidental fires to determine where and how the fire started and how it spread. This is important information because it can be used to prevent similar fires in the future.

Fire investigators also interview witnesses, obtain statements and other necessary documentation, and preserve and examine physical and circumstantial evidence. They tour fire scenes and examine debris to collect evidence, and when possible, arrive at the fire while it is still burning to observe any distinguishing characteristics of the blaze that might help them with their investigation. Fire investigators prepare comprehensive reports, provide detailed accounts of investigative procedures, and present findings. They apprehend and arrest arson suspects, as well as seek confinement and control of fire setters and juveniles who set fires. Fire investigators are often asked to testify in legal proceedings about their investigations and findings. Fire inspectors also prepare damage estimates for reporting and insurance purposes and compile statistics related to fires and investigations.

REQUIREMENTS

High School
Earning a high school diploma is the first step to becoming a fire investigator. Take classes in physics, chemistry, biology, and mathematics. Speech and English courses will help you polish your communication skills.

Postsecondary Training
Fire investigators must have knowledge of fire science, chemistry, engineering, and investigative techniques. Some people obtain a degree in fire investigation. However, a fire-related diploma is not always necessary. An engineering certificate with fire-service experience is sufficient in many cases, depending on the job description and whether the position is in the private (corporate) or public (fire department) sector. Others have degrees in criminal justice. In addition to training at colleges and universities, many fire investigators hone their skills by enrolling in fire investigator training programs and classes offered by professional associations and organizations

A fire investigator picks through the rubble at the scene of The Station nightclub fire in West Warwick, Rhode Island, where 97 people died. *(Joe Giblin, AP Photo)*

such as the National Fire Academy and the International Association of Arson Investigators.

Many fire investigators begin training for the field by becoming firefighters. Many junior and community colleges offer two-year fire-technology programs. Courses involve the study of physics and hydraulics as they apply to pump and nozzle pressures. Fundamentals of chemistry are taught to provide an understanding of chemical methods of extinguishing fires. Skill in communications—both written and spoken—is also emphasized. Beginning firefighters may receive six to 12 or more weeks of intensive training, either as on-the-job training or through formal fire department training schools. Training is given both in the classroom and in the field, where new firefighters are taught the fundamentals of fire fighting, fire prevention, ventilation, emergency medical procedures, the use and care of equipment, and general job duties and skills, including search and rescue techniques. Trainees may also be given instruction in local building codes and fire ordinances. After this period, new firefighters generally serve a six-month to one-year probationary apprenticeship. Apprentice firefighters usually start out on the job as ladder handlers or hose handlers and are given additional responsibilities with training and experience.

Fire investigators often complete their training by participating in an internship with experienced investigators.

Certification or Licensing

The main certification process for fire investigators is certified fire investigator, which is administered by the International Association of Arson Investigators. The National Association of Fire Investigators offers the following voluntary certifications: certified fire and explosion investigator, certified fire investigation instructor, and certified vehicle fire investigator. Contact these organizations for more information.

Investigators who work in the private sector must often be licensed by the state in which they are employed. Contact your state's licensing bureau for information on applicable licensing requirements.

Other Requirements

Fire investigators need to be well-organized. They need to keep their notes and diagrams in good order so that they will be able to write reports in a timely and clear manner. Investigators should be in good physical condition to adapt to extreme weather or fire scene conditions and should be able to withstand long hours in unfavorable conditions. Investigators must have a great deal of integrity and no criminal background. Without this, they will not be credible witnesses in court. They should also have good communication skills, the ability to multitask, and have excellent interpersonal skills.

EXPLORING

Although you can't begin investigating fires on your own, you can, nevertheless, become familiar with the fire safety and science field through a number of activities. First, visit the USFA for Citizens section of the U.S. Fire Administration's Web site, http://www.usfa.fema.gov/safety. This source has fire-safety tips, publications, facts about fires, and more. You can also visit the U.S. Fire Administration's main Web page (http://www.usfa.fema.gov) to find information on topics such as the National Fire Academy, data and statistics, and research.

Once you have done some reading on the field, you may want to contact a professional for more information. Your school counselor or a teacher can help arrange for a visit to a local fire department for a tour of the facilities, where you may also have the opportunity to talk with firefighters about their work. An informational interview with a fire investigator can also provide you with insights.

Many fire departments have volunteer programs. Find out if there are any in your area and sign up to volunteer if you meet their requirements. Keep in good physical shape because this is important for any fire-safety professional. You can also add to your skills by taking CPR and first-aid classes.

EMPLOYERS

There are approximately 14,000 fire investigators and inspectors employed in the United States. Fire investigators are employed by local fire departments, individual state fire marshal offices, government agencies (the U.S. Forest Service, the U.S. Bureau of Alcohol, Tobacco, Firearms and Explosives), special investigation units of insurance companies, private investigation firms, and other organizations in private industry. Others work independently as consultants. The majority of fire investigators work in local government. The majority of opportunities for fire investigators are found in big cities with high population density—places where fires more often occur.

STARTING OUT

There is no straight path to becoming a fire investigator, and it is not an entry-level job. Most of the investigators who come from fire departments start out in the fire-prevention bureau. Others come from police departments. Fire investigation is a multidisciplinary field, which requires skills in many areas, including fire fighting, law enforcement, mechanical engineering, mathematics, and chemical engineering.

Professional organizations often provide job listings at their Web sites. Two such associations that offer online job listings are the International Association of Arson Investigators (http://www.firearson.com/jobs/index.asp) and National Association of Fire Investigators (http://www.nafi.org).

ADVANCEMENT

Fire investigators employed by fire departments can rise in rank within the department. Many become lieutenants, captains, and fire marshals within their jurisdictions. Investigators employed in the private sector advance by receiving pay raises, more challenging cases, or managerial responsibilities. Some fire investigators go on to start their own businesses and work as consultants to fire departments, government agencies, and private industry.

EARNINGS

Fire inspectors and investigators earned a median annual salary of $53,030 in 2008, according to the U.S. Department of Labor. Ten percent earned less than $32,680, and the highest paid 10 percent of all inspectors and investigators earned more than $81,550. Fire inspectors and investigators in local government jobs earned approximately $55,690 a year; those in state government earned $48,560. As in all occupations, the experts demand higher salaries, so private sector investigators' salaries can go much higher (to the $100,000+ range) if they work as national expert witnesses.

Salaried fire investigators usually receive benefits such as vacation days, sick leave, health and life insurance, and a savings and pension program. Self-employed investigators must provide their own benefits.

WORK ENVIRONMENT

Fire investigators have a varied work environment They may spend days at a time in the field conducting scene surveys and interviewing involved parties and then spend the next several days or weeks in the office preparing the reports. Fire investigators travel often to scenes of fires, and may have to rush to the site of an ongoing fire to preserve and gather evidence while the fire is still in progress. When working at the scenes of fires, they must take great care in order to avoid injury by fire, smoke, or debris from damaged structures.

OUTLOOK

Employment of fire investigators is expected to grow about as fast as the average for all careers through 2016, according to the U.S. Department of Labor. There will always be fires to investigate, which will create steady demand for fire investigators. This field is constantly being advanced by new technology and remains one of the most interesting occupational segments of the fire service.

FOR MORE INFORMATION

For information on fire investigation, visit
interFIRE Online
http://www.interfire.org

For information on the investigation of arson, contact
International Association of Arson Investigators
2151 Priest Bridge Drive, Suite 25
Crofton, MD 21114-2466
Tel: 410-451-3473
http://www.firearson.com

For industry information, contact
International Association of Bomb Technicians and Investigators
PO Box 160
Goldvein, VA 22720-0160
Tel: 540-752-4533
Email: admin@iabti.org
http://www.iabti.org

For information on certification, contact
National Association of Fire Investigators
857 Tallevast Road
Sarasota, FL 34243-3257
Tel: 877-506-NAFI
http://www.nafi.org

Visit the association's Web site for a list of state fire marshal Web sites.
National Association of State Fire Marshals
1319 F Street, NW, Suite 301
Washington, DC 20004-1140

Tel: 877-996-2736
Email: info@firemarshals.org
http://www.firemarshals.org

The National Fire Academy provides training both at its campus and through distance education. Classes cover fire investigation, forensic evidence collection, and other topics. Visit its Web site for fire statistics and other resources.
National Fire Academy
16825 South Seton Avenue
Emmitsburg, MD 21727-8920
Tel: 301-447-1000
http://www.usfa.fema.gov/nfa

For information on fire-related careers and fire statistics, contact
National Fire Protection Association
1 Batterymarch Park
Quincy, MA 02169-7471
Tel: 617-770-3000
investigations@nfpa.org
http://www.nfpa.org

For information on fire safety and statistics, contact
U.S. Fire Administration
16825 South Seton Avenue
Emmitsburg, MD 21727-8920
Tel: 301-447-1000
http://www.usfa.dhs.gov

Forensic Accountants and Auditors

OVERVIEW

Forensic accountants and auditors, sometimes known as *investigative accountants, investigative auditors,* and *certified fraud examiners,* use accounting principles and theories to support or oppose claims being made in litigation. Like other accountants and auditors, these professionals are trained to analyze and verify financial records. However, forensic accountants and auditors use these skills to identify and document financial wrongdoing. They prepare reports that may be used in criminal and civil trials. The word "forensic" means "suitable for a court of law, public debate, or formal argumentation." There are more than 1.1 million accountants and auditors, a category which includes forensic accountants and auditors, employed in the United States.

HISTORY

People have used accounting and bookkeeping procedures for as long as they have engaged in trade. Records of accounts have been preserved from ancient and medieval times.

Modern bookkeeping dates back to the advent of double-entry bookkeeping, a method of tracking the impact of transactions on both a company's assets and profitability. Double-entry bookkeeping was developed in medieval Italy. The earliest known published work about this system was written in 1494 by an Italian monk named Luca Pacioli. Pacioli did not invent the system, but he did summarize principles that remain largely unchanged today.

QUICK FACTS

School Subjects
Business
Mathematics

Personal Skills
Communication/ideas
Leadership/management

Work Environment
Primarily indoors
One location with some
  travel

Minimum Education Level
Bachelor's degree

Salary Range
$28,862 to $59,430 to
  $208,000+

Certification or Licensing
Recommended

Outlook
Faster than the average

DOT
160

GOE
04.04.02

NOC
1111

O*NET-SOC
13-2011.00

Records preserved from 16th century Europe indicate that formulations were developed during that time to account for assets, liabilities, and income. When the industrial revolution swept through the world in the 18th century, accounting became even more sophisticated to accommodate the acceleration of financial transactions caused by mechanization and mass production.

In the 20th and 21st centuries accounting has become a more creative and interesting discipline. Computers now perform many routine computations, while accountants tend to spend more time interpreting the results. Many accountants now hold senior management positions within large organizations. They assess the possible impact of various transactions, mergers, and acquisitions and help companies manage their employees more efficiently.

While people have probably investigated financial records for as long as people have kept accounts, forensic accounting did not emerge as a distinct area of specialty until quite recently. The increased litigation and white-collar crime that emerged in the 1980s (and continues today) has contributed to rapid growth in this field.

THE JOB

Forensic accountants and auditors have all the skills possessed by traditional accountants and auditors. They are trained to compile, verify, and analyze financial records and taxes. They monitor the efficiency of business procedures and management. Unlike traditional accounting and auditing professionals, however, forensic accountants and auditors use their skills to help clients prepare for trials. They follow paper trails of financial documents to prepare reports for clients to use in litigation.

In an investigation, the forensic accountant usually begins by reviewing relevant financial and business documents and interviewing the people involved. He or she also may assemble relevant third-party information, such as economic data for comparable industries or companies. Using the compiled information, the forensic accountant may then calculate the losses or damages caused by any financial violations or errors. Finally, the forensic accountant prepares a detailed report explaining his or her findings and conclusions. This report is intended for use in litigation.

Experts estimate that one in 20 cases go to litigation, but accountants must treat every case as if it is going to trial in order to provide comprehensive information to their employers.

If a case is scheduled to proceed to litigation, the attorneys involved may schedule a deposition. A deposition is a pretrial hearing, in which attorneys from both sides may interview one another's witnesses to gain information about the case. Forensic accountants sometimes help attorneys prepare questions for these depositions. They also are sometimes asked to answer questions in a deposition.

If and when a case finally goes to trial, a forensic accountant also may serve as an expert witness and testify before the court. Forensic accountants may offer testimony regarding the nature of the violation, a person's or company's guilt or innocence, and the amount of the resulting damages. As expert witnesses, forensic accountants must be able to present information in a clear and organized manner. They must be able to explain complicated accounting concepts in a way that can be understood by people who are not in the field. They must be able to explain and defend the methods they used to arrive at their conclusions.

There is no "typical" case for a forensic accountant. Forensic accountants use their skills to investigate a wide variety of situations or violations.

Many insurance companies hire forensic accountants to evaluate claims they suspect may be inflated or fraudulent. If an insured company files a claim for a business interruption loss, for example, the insurance company may hire a forensic accountant to make sure the company's loss was as great as the company claims it was. To make this assessment, the forensic accountant must review the company's past financial records. Before calculating the company's probable loss, the forensic accountant also must consider the current marketplace. If the economy is booming and the market for the company's products or services is hot, the insured's losses may be substantial. If the economy is sluggish, or if the company's product has become obsolete, the losses may be much lower.

Insurance companies also hire forensic accountants to assess claimants' loss of income due to accidents or disability, or property loss to fire, flood, or theft. Occasionally, a claimant may hire a forensic accountant to defend his or her claim or to rebut another forensic accountant's testimony.

Forensic accountants also investigate malpractice claims against accountants or auditors. In these cases, forensic accountants must examine the reports prepared by the accountants and auditors to determine whether they followed accepted procedures. If the forensic accountant does discover an error, he or she also may be required to calculate the financial impact of the discrepancy.

Companies sometimes hire forensic accountants to determine whether employees are taking bribes from vendors or customers in return for offering higher payments or lower prices. Companies also hire forensic accountants to detect insider trading. Insider trading occurs when an employee uses privileged information to make a

Areas of Investigation

- Asset misappropriation
- Bankruptcy fraud
- Check kiting
- Contract and procurement fraud
- Credit card fraud
- Embezzlement
- Employee fraud
- Financial statement fraud
- Insurance claims
- Money laundering
- Securities fraud
- Telemarketing fraud

Source: Association of Certified Fraud Examiners

profit—or helps someone else make a profit—by buying or selling stock. Forensic accountants also assist corporate clients by calculating loss due to breach of contract, patent infringement, and fraud.

Some forensic accountants engage in divorce valuation work. These professionals determine the value of the personal assets, liabilities, pensions, and business holdings of individuals involved in a divorce settlement.

REQUIREMENTS

High School

If you are interested in entering this field, take as many math and computer classes as possible in high school. You also should take any available business classes, because forensic accountants and auditors must understand basic business procedures in order to assess business interruption losses. Forensic accountants and auditors who eventually form their own firms also will need management and administrative skills. Business classes can offer you a solid foundation in these areas.

Writing, speech, and communication classes are extremely useful courses to take. A forensic accountant's value to clients depends entirely on his or her ability to provide credible reports and convincing testimony for trial. For this reason, forensic accountants must be able to write clear, organized reports. They must be able to speak clearly and audibly in courtrooms. They must appear poised and confident when speaking publicly, and they must be able to convey complicated information in comprehensible language.

Postsecondary Training
Once in college, you should major in accounting or major in business administration with a minor in accounting. It is important to remember that you will not graduate from college as a forensic accountant or auditor. You will first work as a general accountant or auditor and then learn the skills necessary to be a forensic accountant or auditor through experience. Also included in your course of study should be computer classes, as well as English or communication classes. In the past several years, a few colleges (such as Carlow University, Franklin University, Mount Marty College, Myers University, and Waynesburg College) have started offering degrees and concentrations in forensic accounting, but most students still prepare for this field by majoring in accounting and learning forensic accounting techniques on the job.

Some organizations prefer to hire accountants and auditors with master's degrees in accounting or master's in business administration. So, depending on what company you want to work for, you may need to continue your education beyond the college level.

Certification or Licensing
Anyone who is interested in becoming a forensic accountant should first become a certified public accountant (CPA). While it is theoretically possible to practice as a forensic accountant without becoming a CPA, it is extremely unlikely that anyone would succeed in so doing. Clients hire forensic accountants with the idea that they may eventually serve as expert witnesses. A forensic accountant who is not certified could be easily discredited in a trial.

To become a CPA, most states require candidates to have completed 150 credit hours, or the equivalent of a master's degree, in an accounting program of study. The American Institute of Certified Public Accountants (AICPA) is working to make this a national standard for accounting education as accounting procedures and reporting laws become increasingly more complex. Candidates for the credential also must pass the Uniform CPA Examination, which is developed by the AICPA. Finally, many states require candidates to have a certain amount of professional experience (usually at least two years) to qualify for certification. Most states also require CPAs to earn about 40 hours of continuing education each year.

AICPA members who have valid CPA certificates may also earn the following specialty designations: accredited in business valuation, certified in financial forensics, certified information technology professional, and personal financial specialist.

A CPA who has gained some experience should consider becoming a certified fraud examiner (CFE). Forensic accountants and fraud examiners use many of the same skills. In fact, the titles are sometimes used interchangeably, although, according to the National Association of Forensic Accountants (NAFA), fraud examiners are more often concerned with developing procedures and implementing measures to prevent fraud. However, the two areas are not mutually exclusive; many forensic accountants also work as fraud examiners and vice versa. To gain the CFE designation, a CPA must meet certain educational and professional experience requirements and pass the Uniform CFE Examination, which is administered by the Association of Certified Fraud Examiners. The designation can help forensic accountants establish their credibility as expert witnesses. CFEs must complete a certain amount of continuing education each year.

The National Association of Forensic Accountants also offers certification to its members. Contact the association for more information.

Other Requirements
Forensic accountants and auditors are the sleuths of the financial world. Consequently, they must be curious and dogged in their pursuit of answers. They must have exceptional attention to detail and be capable of intense concentration. Like every professional involved with the judicial system, forensic accountants and auditors are frequently subject to abrupt schedule changes, so they also should be able to work under stressful conditions and meet exceptionally tight deadlines. They also must have excellent communication skills and they must be poised and confident.

EXPLORING

Opportunities for high school students to explore this field are limited. You may, however, contact people in this field to request information interviews. Information interviews can be an excellent way to learn about different careers. You can also visit Web sites that provide information on accounting. The American Institute of Certified Public Accountants offers an excellent Web site called Start Here, Go Places in Business and Accounting (http://www.startherego places.com) that provides information on careers, educational training, scholarships, internships, and the CPA Examination.

Hone your math skills outside of the classroom by joining your high school math team or by volunteering as a math tutor at your school or a local learning center. You can also improve your business and accounting skills by joining a school group that has a yearly budget and offering to be the treasurer. This will give you the opportunity to be responsible for an organization's financial records.

Try landing a summer job performing clerical tasks for accounting or law firms. This experience can help you become familiar with the documentation necessary in both fields. When in college, you should seek internship positions within accounting firms in order to gain practical experience and to make contacts within the industry.

EMPLOYERS

More than 1.1 million accountants and auditors (a category that includes forensic accountants and auditors) are employed in the United States. Forensic accountants and auditors usually work for accounting companies that provide litigation support for insurance companies, law firms, and other parties involved in litigation.

STARTING OUT

Most people spend several years working as accountants before specializing in forensic accounting. Their first hurdle after college is to find employment as an accountant. College professors and career services counselors can help accounting majors arrange interviews with respected accounting firms and government agencies. Students also can contact these firms and agencies directly to learn about job opportunities. Many accounting firms and government positions are advertised in newspapers and on the Internet.

In general, accounting firms tend to offer better starting salaries than government agencies. Larger firms also sometimes have entire departments dedicated to litigation support services. New graduates who secure positions with these firms might have opportunities to learn the forensic ropes while gaining experience as accountants. With time, after earning a CPA and gaining experience, an accountant within a large firm may have an opportunity to specialize in litigation support and forensic accounting. The largest firms include PricewaterhouseCoopers, Ernst & Young, Deloitte Touche Tohmatsu, and KPMG International.

Another excellent way to gain relevant experience is by working for the Internal Revenue Service (IRS). IRS auditors and accountants use many of the same skills necessary for forensic accountants.

ADVANCEMENT

Forensic accountants and auditors usually advance by gaining experience and establishing reputations for integrity, thorough documentation, and reliable calculations. As a forensic accountant or auditor gains experience, he or she usually attracts more clients and is able to work on more interesting, complex cases. Experienced forensic accountants and auditors also can charge more per hour for their services, though, unless the individual is self-employed, this increase does not usually benefit the professional directly. With experience, forensic accountants and auditors also may gain opportunities to manage a litigation support department or to become a partner in an accounting firm. A significant number of forensic accountants and auditors also advance by leaving larger firms to establish their own companies.

EARNINGS

While there are no annual salary statistics specifically for forensic accountants and auditors, most of these professionals work within accounting firms and earn salaries that are commensurate with those of other accountants and auditors. According to the U.S. Department of Labor, the median annual earnings for accountants and auditors as a whole were $59,430 in 2008. The top 10 percent of accountants and auditors earned more than $102,380, and the bottom 10 percent earned less than $36,720.

According to a survey conducted by the National Association of Colleges and Employers, entry-level public sector accountants who had bachelor's degrees received average starting salaries of $50,403 in 2008. Those in the private sector earned $46,684. Auditors in the public sector earned average starting salaries of $49,680, while those who worked in the private sector earned $48,228.

General accountants and internal auditors with up to one year of experience earned between $31,500 and $48,250, according to a 2007 survey by Robert Half International. Some experienced auditors may earn between $60,000 and $208,000, depending on such factors as their education level, the size of the firm, and the firm's location. Partners in accounting firms can make even more. Naturally, salaries are affected by such factors as size of the firm, the level of the individual's education, and any certification he or she may have.

Government positions typically offer somewhat lower salaries than other positions. According to the U.S. Department of Labor, the average starting annual salary for junior accountants and auditors in the federal government was $28,862 in 2007. Candidates who had master's degrees or two years of experience could earn $43,731 to start. More experienced accountants in the federal government made about $78,665 per year in 2007.

As forensic accountants become more experienced, they may earn slightly more than traditional accountants because many firms tend to charge premium rates for litigation support services. A forensic accountant's salary and bonus figures usually reflect, at least to some degree, the revenue they are generating for the accounting firm. For this reason, a forensic accountant's salary tends to grow as he or she gains experience. According to the National Association of Forensic Accountants, forensic accountants who had fewer than 10 years of experience charged between $80 and $140 per hour for their services. About 25 percent of those who had 11 to 15 years of experience charged between $141 and $170 per hour, and another 25 percent charged more than $170. Practitioners with between 16 and 20 years of experience charged between $171 and $200. In addition, 30 percent of those with more than 20 years of experience charged more than $200.

Most forensic accountants and auditors are employees who receive standard benefits such as paid vacation and sick days, health insurance, and 401(k) savings plans. Many who work for major accounting firms can also expect to earn bonuses based on their performance and the overall performance of their firm. Forensic accountants and auditors who become partners also may earn shares in the firm. Forensic accountants and auditors who act as self-employed consultants typically will not receive benefits and will have to provide their own health insurance and retirement plan.

WORK ENVIRONMENT

Forensic accountants and auditors typically work in bright, clean offices. A great deal of their work is done on computers and telephones, though most also occasionally travel to the offices of clients or those under investigation.

Because forensic accountants and auditors are hired to help clients prepare for trial, they often must work under tremendous pressure. They frequently encounter tight deadlines and changing schedules. Though forensic accountants and auditors generally work normal 40-hour weeks, they often work much longer hours as they prepare for a trial.

Forensic accountants and auditors also must contend with the pressures of serving as expert witnesses. Whenever they take the stand, they know that the attorneys for the other side of a case will attempt to discredit them and question their procedures and conclusions. Forensic accountants and auditors must be prepared to undergo extremely aggressive questioning. They must be able to remain calm and confident under trying circumstances.

OUTLOOK

The U.S. Department of Labor predicts that employment for accountants and auditors will grow faster than the average for all occupations through 2016. As the economy grows, more accountants will be needed to prepare books and taxes for new and growing companies. New accountants also will be needed to replace those who retire or change professions. Since more than 1.1 million people currently work as accountants, the number of positions created by normal turnover should be significant.

The AICPA and the U.S. Department of Labor call forensic accounting one of the hot growth areas for CPAs. One reason for this may be that the job is becoming well known due to high profile cases of financial mismanagement by formerly respected accounting firms such as Arthur Andersen. In this case, forensic accountants were among the experts that investigated the financial collapse of the previously stable company Enron and determined that obstruction of justice was committed by Arthur Andersen employees.

In our increasingly complex economy of business mergers, acquisitions, and failures, forensic accountants and auditors are increasingly in demand as companies rely on their services to determine if bankruptcy should be declared or if there is a way to remain solvent. The NAFA notes that the need for investigative accountants continues to increase in proportion to the insurance industry's growth and complexity. This is because insurance companies use these accountants' skills when determining how to settle claims, such as for business interruptions, inventory damage or loss, or any type of insurance claim where fraud may occur. Due to this demand, the overall outlook for forensic accountants and auditors should be good.

FOR MORE INFORMATION

For information on forensic careers and education, contact
American Academy of Forensic Sciences
410 North 21st Street
Colorado Springs, CO 80904-2712
Tel: 719-636-1100
http://www.aafs.org

Because forensic accountants are almost always certified public accountants, the institute is an excellent source of additional information.

American Institute of Certified Public Accountants
1211 Avenue of the Americas
New York, NY 10036-8775
http://www.aicpa.org

For information on careers, The Fraud Museum, scholarships, self-study courses, and the CFE designation, contact

Association of Certified Fraud Examiners
The Gregor Building
716 West Avenue
Austin, TX 78701-2727
Tel: 800-245-3321
Email: accounting@ACFE.com
http://www.cfenet.com

For information on investigative accounting, contact

National Association of Forensic Accountants
6451 North Federal Highway, Suite 121
Fort Lauderdale, FL 33308-1487
Tel: 800-523-3680
Email: mail@nafanet.com
http://www.nafanet.com

For information on membership, scholarships for college students, and continuing education, contact

National Society of Accountants
1010 North Fairfax Street
Alexandria, VA 22314-1504
Tel: 800-966-6679
http://www.nsacct.org

Forensic Anthropologists

QUICK FACTS

School Subjects
Geography
History

Personal Skills
Communication/ideas
Helping/teaching

Work Environment
Indoors and outdoors
One location with some
 travel

Minimum Education Level
Doctorate degree

Salary Range
$32,150 to $53,910 to
 $117,700+

Certification or Licensing
Recommended

Outlook
More slowly than the average

DOT
054

GOE
11.03.03

NOC
4169

O*NET-SOC
19-3091.00, 19-3091.01,
 25-1061.00

OVERVIEW

Forensic anthropologists examine and identify bones and skeletal remains for the purposes of homicide, scientific, archaeological, or judicial investigations. Forensic anthropology is a branch of physical, or biological, anthropology. There are approximately 5,200 anthropologists employed in the United States. Only a very small percentage of anthropologists specialize in forensic anthropology.

HISTORY

Forensic anthropology is a relatively new scientific discipline. Thomas Dwight is considered to be the father of forensic anthropology. He was an anatomist and educator at Harvard College, Bowdoin College, and Harvard Medical School. At Harvard's Warren Museum of Anatomy, Dwight created a section on osteology, the study of human bones. He developed an international reputation as an anatomist and wrote several books on the field including *Frozen Sections of a Child* (1872) and *Clinical Atlas of Variations of the Bones of the Hands and Feet* (1907). But despite Dwight's early work in the field, it wasn't until the 1930s that police and organizations began turning to physical anthropologists to help solve grisly murders, which were often perpetuated by organized crime gangs.

The field underwent major advances during World War II and the Korean War. Hundreds of thousands of soldiers were killed during action, and forensic anthropologists were needed to identify the dead using health information gathered from the soldiers before they shipped off to battle.

Today, forensic anthropologists are in demand to help law enforcement agencies, human rights groups, government agencies, and other organizations identify human remains and solve crimes and identify victims of accidents, suicide, or natural disasters.

THE JOB

Forensic anthropologists examine human bones and skeletal remains to help identify the person to whom they belonged. When people lose their lives in tragedies such as plane crashes, fires, or terrorist attacks, sometimes the only part of their bodies that is left intact is bone.

A forensic anthropologist with the Joint POW/MIA Accounting Command attempts to put together skull remains in order to help identify a serviceman killed during World War II. *(Lucy Pemoni, AP Photo)*

Forensic anthropologists assist in the collection of remains from crime (ranging from a single murder to genocide) or accident scenes, clean up the bones to make analysis easier, and patiently examine and study the bones for any possible identifying information.

After first making sure that the bones being examined are those of a human, forensic anthropologists make observations and measurements, using tools such as magnifying glasses, microscopes, and calipers, that can give them a great deal of information about whose bones they are studying. This information can include the person's gender (there is a weight and size difference between male and female bones), age (less-complete bone development indicates a younger person, evidence of arthritis points to someone older), race (via known differences in nose and eye socket structure among different races), height and body type (which can be calculated based on the size of specific bones), and other unique features. Data from this type of analysis, when checked against information on missing-persons lists, played an important part in helping police identify many of the victims of serial killer John Wayne Gacy in the late 1970s.

Forensic anthropologists can be of further assistance to law enforcement officials in determining a person's cause of death, if trauma from a bullet or stab wound has affected a bone. Those with additional knowledge of *forensic entomology* (the scientific study of insect evidence) can also help pinpoint the time of death. (For more information, see the article, Forensic Entomologists.) Some forensic anthropologists specialize in facial reproduction, which is the art of attempting to re-create the appearance of a person's face.

Many forensic anthropologists are employed by academic or research institutions and are called in to work on cases when tragedies such as plane crashes, terrorist attacks, or natural disasters occur. Others work for medical examiner's offices or for the military. Forensic anthropologists are also often called upon to testify in court about their findings.

REQUIREMENTS

High School

Follow your high school's college prep program to be prepared for undergraduate and graduate programs in anthropology. You should study English composition and literature to develop your writing and interpretation skills. Foreign language skills will also help you in later research and language study. Take classes in computers and classes in sketching, simple surveying, and photography to prepare for some of the demands of field work. Mathematics and science courses can help you develop the skills you'll need in analyzing information and statistics.

Participation in science clubs and competitions will give you a general introduction to the scientific terms, investigative techniques, and laboratory practices that are used by scientists.

Postsecondary Training

You should be prepared for a long training period beyond high school. Most forensic anthropologists have a doctorate in anthropology with an emphasis on the study of human anatomy and osteology. This course of study requires about four to 10 years of work beyond the bachelor's degree. You'll also need a doctorate in order to join the faculty of college and university anthropology programs. Before beginning graduate work, you will study such basic courses as psychology, sociology, history, geography, mathematics, logic, English composition, and literature, as well as modern and ancient languages. The final two years of the undergraduate program will provide an opportunity for specialization not only in anthropology but in some specific phase of the discipline (in this instance, forensic science).

Students planning to become forensic anthropologists should concentrate on biological or physical anthropology and focus on skeletal biology, human anatomy, statistics, and archaeological recovery methods.

In starting graduate training, you should select an institution that has a good program in the area in which you hope to specialize. This is important, not only because the training should be of a high quality, but because most graduates in anthropology will receive their first jobs through their graduate universities. The American Association of Physical Anthropologists offers a list of graduate programs in anthropology at its Web site (http://www.physanth. org/departmental-graduate-programs-in-physical-anthropology). Assistantships and temporary positions may be available to holders of bachelor's or master's degrees, but are usually available only to those working toward a doctorate.

Because this type of work may be sporadic, students interested in the profession should seek to ensure that they have other career options by obtaining an undergraduate education that covers a wide range of topics in physical anthropology.

Certification or Licensing

The American Board of Forensic Anthropology awards certification to forensic anthropologists who have a Ph.D., demonstrate experience in the field, and pass a practical and written examination. Contact the board for more information.

Other Requirements

You should be able to work as part of a team, as well as conduct research entirely on your own. Forensic anthropologists often work with forensic pathologists, odontologists, and homicide investigators on a case. Because much of your career will involve study and research, you should have great curiosity and a desire for knowledge. Forensic anthropologists who testify in court need excellent communication skills. All workers need good writing skills in order to document their findings.

EXPLORING

General anthropology may be explored in a number of ways. Local amateur anthropological societies may have weekly or monthly meetings and guest speakers, study developments in the field, and engage in exploration on the local level.

Trips to museums also will introduce you to the world of anthropology. Both high school and college students may work in museums on a part-time basis during the school year or during summer vacations.

If you are interested in forensic anthropology, you should read books and periodicals about the field. Ask your science teacher to arrange an information interview with a forensic anthropologist. You can also learn more about this interesting field by visiting ForensicAnthro.com (http://www.forensicanthro.com).

EMPLOYERS

Approximately 5,200 anthropologists are employed in the United States; forensic anthropologists make up only a very small percentage of this total. Forensic anthropologists are employed by research institutions, colleges and universities, medical examiner's offices, law enforcement agencies, human rights organizations, and the military. Anthropologists who work outside the field of forensic anthropology work for educational institutions, museums, social service programs, health organizations, city planning departments, and marketing departments of corporations. Most forensic anthropologists are employed as independent consultants.

STARTING OUT

The most promising way to gain entry into this occupation is through graduate school. Graduates in anthropology might be approached prior to graduation by prospective employers. Often, professors will provide you with introductions as well as recommendations. You may have an opportunity to work as a research assistant or a teaching fellow while in graduate school, and frequently this experience is of tremendous help in qualifying for a job in another institution.

You should also be involved in internships to gain experience. These internship opportunities may be available through your graduate program, or you may have to seek them out yourself. Many organizations can benefit from the help of an anthropology student; health centers, government agencies, and human rights groups all conduct research.

Additionally, many professional associations offer job listings at their Web sites. Visit the Web sites of the American Anthropological Association (http://www.aaanet.org/profdev) and the American Association of Physical Anthropologists (http://www.physanth.org) for job listings.

ADVANCEMENT

Advancement may be somewhat limited because the field of anthropology is very small. Most people beginning their teaching careers in colleges or universities will start as instructors and eventually advance to assistant professor, associate professor, and possibly full professor. Researchers on the college level have an opportunity to head research areas and to gain recognition among colleagues as an expert in many areas of study. Anthropologists employed in museums also have an opportunity to advance within the institution in terms of raises in salary or increases in responsibility and job prominence. Those anthropologists working outside academia and museums will be promoted according to the standards of the individual companies and organizations for which they work.

The field of forensic anthropology is very small, and many forensic anthropologists work part time. Advancement for forensic anthropologists who are salaried employees typically involves increases in salary and job duties. Self-employed forensic anthropologists can advance by becoming recognized experts in the field, and be asked to work on high-profile cases.

EARNINGS

The U.S. Department of Labor does not provide salary information for forensic anthropologists, but it does offer information on earnings for anthropology professors and anthropologists employed in all fields (including forensic anthropology). According to the U.S. Department of Labor, college and university anthropology professors earned between $39,290 and $117,700 in 2008, depending on the type of institution. The median salary for these professors was $62,820.

For those working outside of academia, the salaries vary widely. The U.S. Department of Labor reports that the median annual salary for all anthropologists and archeologists was $53,910 in 2008. Salaries ranged from less than $32,150 to $89,490 or more. Forensic anthropologists who work as consultants typically earn $100 to $200 an hour. Benefits for full-time workers include vacation and sick time, health, and sometimes dental, insurance, and pension or 401(k) plans. Self-employed forensic anthropologists must provide their own benefits.

WORK ENVIRONMENT

The majority of forensic anthropologists are employed by colleges and universities, medical examiner's offices, and law enforcement agencies and, as such, have good working conditions, although field work may require extensive travel and difficult living conditions. Educational facilities are normally clean, well lighted, and ventilated.

Full-time forensic anthropologists work about 40 hours a week, and the hours may be irregular. Forensic anthropologists must be able to handle unpleasant sights and smells such as decomposing flesh, trauma to the human body, bodily fluids, and maggots and other insects. Physical strength and stamina is necessary for field work. Those working on excavations of mass graves, for instance, may work during most of the daylight hours and spend the evening planning the next day's activities. Those engaged in teaching may spend many hours in laboratory research or in preparing lessons to be taught. The work is interesting, however, and those employed in the field are usually highly motivated and unconcerned about long, irregular hours or primitive living conditions.

OUTLOOK

The field of forensic anthropology is extremely small. As a result, employment in the field will grow very slowly as a result of low turnover in the profession. Advances in technology and testing procedures may create more opportunities for forensic anthropologists in the future as more agencies seek their skills to help solve cases.

Although college and university teaching has been the largest area of employment for all types of anthropologists, it will still be difficult to land a job in this highly competitive employment area. Overall, the number of job applicants will be greater than the number of openings available. Competition will be great even for those with doctorates who are seeking faculty positions, and many will find only temporary or nontenured jobs. The U.S. Department of Labor predicts that employment for anthropologists who are employed in all fields will grow faster than the average for all occupations through 2016.

FOR MORE INFORMATION

For information on forensic careers, education, and its membership section for physical anthropologists, contact
American Academy of Forensic Sciences
410 North 21st Street
Colorado Springs, CO 80904-2712
Tel: 719-636-1100
http://www.aafs.org

The following organization offers valuable information about anthropological careers and student associations:
American Anthropological Association
2200 Wilson Boulevard, Suite 600
Arlington, VA 22201-3357
Tel: 703-528-1902
http://www.aaanet.org

For information on graduate training in anthropology, contact
American Association of Physical Anthropologists
http://www.physanth.org

For information on certification, contact
American Board of Forensic Anthropology
http://www.theabfa.org

For information on forensic science, contact
American College of Forensic Examiners
2750 East Sunshine Street
Springfield, MO 65804-2047
800-423-9737
http://www.acfei.com

Forensic Biologists

QUICK FACTS

School Subjects
Biology
Speech

Personal Skills
Technical/scientific

Work Environment
Indoors and outdoors
Primarily multiple locations

Minimum Education Level
Bachelor's degree

Salary Range
$35,620 to $65,080 to
$101,030+

Certification or Licensing
Voluntary

Outlook
About as fast as the average

DOT
041

GOE
02.03.03

NOC
2121

O*NET-SOC
19-1020.01, 19-1029.00

OVERVIEW

Biologists study the origin, development, anatomy, function, distribution, and other basic principles of living organisms. They are concerned with the nature of life itself in humans, microorganisms, plants, and animals, and with the relationship of each organism to its environment. *Forensic biologists* are specialized biologists who employ scientific principles and methods to analyze biological specimens so they can be used as evidence in a court of law.

HISTORY

Biological materials—such as blood and other bodily fluids, and bones, hair, nails, skin, and other bodily tissues—has been used informally for hundreds, if not thousands, of years, to convict or acquit the accused. But forensic biology as we know it today can only be traced back to the 1830s. The first procedures for the microscopic detection of sperm were published in 1839, according to the Forensic Science Timeline, a Web site by Norah Rudin and Keith Inman. In 1853 the German histologist Ludwig Teichmann developed a test for the presence of blood.

In the following years, new tests, investigative methods, and scientific equipment were developed, which created a demand for formalized settings where evidence could be studied. In 1910 the first police crime laboratory was founded at the University of Lyons in France. The first forensic laboratory in the U.S. was founded in 1923 in Los Angeles, California. In 1932 the Federal Bureau of Investigation crime lab was created. Also in the 1930s biological evidence was used to solve the kidnapping and murder of aviator Charles Lindbergh's baby boy. Wood from a homemade ladder left at the crime scene was matched with wood from the home of the individual who was accused of the crime. This was the first time that forensic botanical evidence, a branch of forensics biology, was accepted in an American court.

The field of forensic biology experienced major advances in 1944 when Oswald Avery and a team of scientists were able to isolate and identify DNA as the transmitter of genetic information. In 1953 James Watson, Francis Crick, and Maurice Wilkins deciphered the complex structure of DNA and predicted that it carried the genetic code for all living matter. The first DNA profiling test was developed in 1984, and in 1987 DNA profiling was used for the first time to catch a murderer and exonerate an individual accused of a crime (both during the same investigation). Today DNA testing has become one of the major tools of forensic biologists, who continue to use this and other methods to help solve crimes.

THE JOB

Forensic biologists analyze biological materials, such as blood, saliva, and other bodily fluids, bones, hair, nails, skin, and other bodily tissue. They may also work with nonhuman-based biological samples, such as those from plants or animals. It is the responsibility of the forensic biologist to analyze the biological material using various laboratory procedures and document their findings so they can be presented as evidence in legal proceedings.

Some forensic biologists work at crime scenes to identify and collect biological specimens that can be used as evidence, but most forensic biologists primarily work in a laboratory, handling biological material that has already been collected and delivered to them. A forensic biologist employs different methods to study and analyze biological evidence. Biological samples must first be catalogued and photographed, if this was not already done before they reached the forensic biologist. The samples may be viewed by high-magnification instruments, such as microscopes, and/or subjected to any number of biological-based test or procedures. DNA analysis—where DNA genetic markers from biological evidence collected at a crime scene are compared to DNA markers in other samples—is one such method used by forensic biologists. DNA analysis can establish whether any of the biological evidence collected at a crime scene could have come from a suspect in the case at hand, or if it matches any of the entries in CODIS (Combined DNA Index System), the national DNA databank maintained by the Federal Bureau of Investigation. Depending on what type of biological sample is being analyzed and the type of test that is used, forensic biologists can sometimes determine many characteristics useful to a criminal investigation, such as the sex, age, or other descriptors of the person (or animal, as the case may be) from whom the biological sample was obtained.

Because the biological samples being analyzed are primarily intended to be used as evidence in a court of law, forensic biologists must take great care to carefully handle the samples, take detailed notes about how and what was done to them through the course of any tests or procedures, and prepare clear but thorough reports that document their findings. This must be done to ensure that important evidence is allowed to be used for consideration in legal proceedings, rather than being dismissed for such reasons as the fact that a forensic biologist forgot to document part of a test, a sample was not maintained at the proper temperature, or evidence was misplaced due to inappropriate cataloguing procedures. Many forensic biologists testify in court regarding their findings or to explain the science so that people without a background in science can understand the relevance of the biological evidence.

Some forensic biologists routinely work with nonhuman based samples. They might be involved in investigations of animal abuse, outbreaks of disease in a specific animal population, or illegal activity connected to endangered species. They might also be involved in investigating environmental contaminants or threats to public health.

Although most forensic biologists are civilian workers, some are sworn law enforcement officers.

REQUIREMENTS

High School

High school students interested in a career in forensic biology should take English, biology, physics, chemistry, Latin, geometry, and algebra.

Postsecondary Training

You will need a minimum of a bachelor's degree in biology, microbiology, biochemistry, forensic science, chemistry, or a related field to work as a forensic biologist. Prospective forensic biologists should also obtain a broad undergraduate college training. In addition to courses in all phases of biology, useful related courses include organic and inorganic chemistry, molecular biology, biochemistry, physics, and mathematics. Modern languages, English, biometrics (the use of mathematics in biological measurements), and statistics are also useful. Courses in computers will be extremely beneficial. Students should take advantage of courses that require laboratory, field, or collecting work. Important coursework for those who want to specialize in DNA analysis include genetics, molecular biology, statistics, and biochemistry.

Nearly all postsecondary institutions offer undergraduate training in one or more of the biological sciences. These vary from liberal arts schools that offer basic majors in botany and zoology to large universities that permit specialization in areas such as entomology, bacteriology, and physiology at the undergraduate level.

For the highest professional status, a doctorate is required. This is particularly true of top research positions and most higher-level college teaching openings. Many colleges and universities offer courses leading to a master's degree and a doctorate.

The American Academy of Forensic Sciences offers a list of colleges and universities that offer degrees in forensic biology and related fields at its Web site (http://www.aafs.org).

New forensic biologists typically participate in on-the-job training that lasts from six months to two years. They also continue to learn throughout their careers by participating in seminars, workshops, and other educational activities.

Certification or Licensing

The International Association for Identification offers several certification categories that may be of interest to forensic biologists, including certified crime scene analyst and bloodstain pattern examiner certification. Contact the association for more information.

The American College of Forensic Examiners offers the certified forensic consultant program, which provides an overview of the U.S. judicial system, and would be a good option for forensic biologists who testify in court. Contact the college for more information.

Other Requirements

Forensic biologists must be systematic in their approach to collecting and analyzing evidence. They should have probing, inquisitive minds and an aptitude for biology, chemistry, and mathematics. Patience and imagination are also required since they may spend much time analyzing evidence and data. Forensic biologists must also have good communication skills in order to effectively gather and exchange data and solve problems that arise in their work. These skills will especially come in handy for those who testify in court.

EXPLORING

You can measure your aptitude and interest in the work of biologists by taking courses in the field. Laboratory assignments, for example, provide information on techniques used by the working biologist. Many schools hire students as laboratory assistants to work directly under a teacher and help administer the laboratory sections of courses.

School assemblies, field trips to government and private crime laboratories and research centers, and career conferences provide additional insight into career opportunities. Advanced students often are able to attend professional meetings and seminars.

Part-time and summer positions in biology or related areas are particularly helpful. Students with some college courses in biology may find summer positions as laboratory assistants. Graduate students may find work on research projects conducted by their institutions. Beginning college and advanced high school students may find employment as laboratory aides or hospital orderlies or attendants. Despite the menial nature of these positions, they afford a useful insight into careers in biology. High school students often have the opportunity to join volunteer service groups at local hospitals. Student science training programs (SSTPs) allow qualified high school students to spend a summer doing research under the supervision of a scientist. They can also participate in biology-related summer experience programs and camps at colleges and universities.

You can also ask your science teacher to arrange an interview with a forensic biologist, read books about the field (such as *Essential Forensic Biology,* by Alan Gunn), surf the Web to learn more about forensic biology, and attend court proceedings that feature testimony by forensic biologists.

EMPLOYERS

Forensic biologists work at forensic science laboratories at various governmental levels. They also work for law firms and in academia. Biologists who do not specialize in forensic biology are employed by government agencies, pharmaceutical companies, hospitals, biotechnology companies, laboratories, and a wide variety of other employers.

STARTING OUT

Forensic biologists should apply directly to forensic science laboratories for employment opportunities. Governmental agencies that employ forensic biologists often interview college seniors on campus. Private and public employment offices frequently have listings from these employers. Opportunities may also be found through college career services offices and through contacts made while participating in internships.

Special application procedures are required for positions with government agencies. Civil service applications for federal, state, and municipal positions may be obtained by writing to the agency involved and from high school and college career services offices and public employment agencies.

ADVANCEMENT

With the right qualifications, the forensic biologist may advance to the position of project chief and direct a team of other forensic biologists. Many use their knowledge and experience as background for administrative and management positions. Often, as they develop professional expertise, forensic biologists move from strictly technical assignments into positions in which they interpret biological knowledge.

Some forensic biologists become technical specialists in a field such as DNA analysis. Others move on to larger agencies or more prestigious cases. Some become college professors or educators at other academic levels.

EARNINGS

There is no comprehensive salary information available for forensic biologists. The U.S. Department of Labor does provide information on biologists, not otherwise classified (a category that includes forensic biologists). The median salary for these professionals was $65,080 in 2008. Salaries ranged from less than $35,620 to $101,030 or more. In 2008 biological scientists working for the federal government earned a mean annual salary of $70,270, and those employed by state government agencies earned $55,500. Earnings for forensic biologists vary extensively based on the type and size of their employer, the individual's level of education and experience, and other factors.

Forensic biologists are usually eligible for health and dental insurance, paid vacations and sick days, and retirement plans. Some employers may offer reimbursement for continuing education, seminars, and travel.

WORK ENVIRONMENT

The forensic biologist's work environment varies greatly depending upon the position and type of employer. One forensic biologist may frequently travel to and work at crime scenes and may be required to move bodies or investigative equipment. Another spends most of his or her time working in a laboratory. Many forensic biologists work with toxic substances, human tissues and fluids, and potentially harmful chemicals and disease cultures; strict safety measures must be observed. Some must testify in court and participate in recorded depositions. Courtrooms can sometimes be tense and stressful places, and forensic biologists should be able to defend their findings under sometimes harsh questioning from defense attorneys or other individuals involved in the case.

OUTLOOK

The U.S. Department of Labor predicts that employment for biological scientists will grow about as fast as the average for all careers through 2016, although competition will be stiff for some positions. For example, Ph.D.'s looking for research positions will find strong competition for a limited number of openings. In addition, certain government jobs as well as government funding for research may also be less plentiful. A recession or shift in political power can cause the loss of funding for forensic science laboratories. Biologists with advanced degrees will be best qualified for the most lucrative and challenging jobs, although this varies by specialty, with genetic, cellular, and biochemical research showing the most promise. Scientists with bachelor's degrees may find openings as science or engineering technicians or as health technologists and technicians. Many colleges and universities are cutting back on their faculties, but high schools and two-year colleges may have teaching positions available.

Employment opportunities should also be strong for those who specialize in forensic biology. There have been major developments in evidence analysis (especially DNA) in the past 25 years, and these new techniques have created demand for forensic biologists. Opportunities should be best for experienced forensic biologists with advanced training in the field.

FOR MORE INFORMATION

For information on forensic careers and education, contact
American Academy of Forensic Sciences
410 North 21st Street
Colorado Springs, CO 80904-2712
Tel: 719-636-1100
http://www.aafs.org

For information on forensic science and certification, contact
American College of Forensic Examiners
2750 East Sunshine Street
Springfield, MO 65804-2047
Tel: 800-423-9737
http://www.acfei.com

For information on careers in biology, contact
American Institute of Biological Sciences
1444 I Street, NW, Suite 200
Washington, DC 20005-6535
Tel: 202-628-1500
http://www.aibs.org

For more information on physiology, contact
American Physiological Society
9650 Rockville Pike
Bethesda, MD 20814-3991
Tel: 301-634-7164
http://www.the-aps.org

For information on careers, educational resources, and fellowships,
contact
American Society for Microbiology
1752 N Street, NW
Washington, DC 20036-2904
Tel: 202-737-3600
http://www.asm.org

For general information about plant biology, contact
American Society of Plant Biologists
http://www.aspb.org

For useful forensic science Web links, visit the association's Web site.
Association of Forensic DNA Analysts and Administrators
PO Box 4983
Austin, TX 78765-4983
http://www.afdaa.org

For career information, including articles and books, contact
Biotechnology Industry Organization
1201 Maryland Avenue, SW, Suite 900
Washington, DC 20024-2149

Tel: 202-962-9200
Email: info@bio.org
http://www.bio.org

To learn more about forensic services at the FBI, visit the FBI Laboratory Division's Web site.
Federal Bureau of Investigation (FBI)
J. Edgar Hoover Building
935 Pennsylvania Avenue, NW
Washington, DC 20535-0001
Tel: 202-324-3000
http://www.fbi.gov/hq/lab/labhome.htm

For information on certification, contact
International Association for Identification
2535 Pilot Knob Road, Suite 117
Mendota Heights, MN 55120-1120
Tel: 651-681-8566
http://www.theiai.org

For information about the field, contact
International Society for Forensic Genetics
http://www.isfg.org

For information on specific careers in biology (including forensic biology), contact
National Institutes of Health
9000 Rockville Pike
Bethesda, MD 20892-0001
Tel: 301-496-4000
Email: NIHinfo@od.nih.gov
http://www.nih.gov

Forensic Botanists

OVERVIEW

Botanists study all different aspects of plant life, from cell structure to reproduction, to how plants are distributed, to how rainfall or other conditions affect them, and more. *Forensic botanists* are botanists with specialized training who collect and analyze plant material found at crime scenes. Only a small number of botanists specialize in forensic botany.

HISTORY

Plant science is hundreds of years old. The invention of microscopes in the 1600s was very important to the development of modern botany. Microscopes allowed minute study of plant anatomy and cells and led to considerable research in the field. It was in the 1600s that people started using words like botanographist or botanologist, or one who describes plants. In the 1700s Carolus Linnaeus, a Swedish botanist and taxonomist (one who identifies, names, and classifies plants) was an important figure. He came up with the two-name (genus and species) system for describing plants that is still used today. In all, Linnaeus wrote more than 180 works on plants, plant diseases, and related subjects.

No one knows for sure when botanical evidence was used for the first time to solve a crime. Forensic botany as a professional discipline has been around for less than 100 years. One of the first recorded instances of the use of forensic botany in a legal proceeding occurred in 1932, in response to the kidnapping of the baby boy of the famous aviator Charles Lindbergh. (The boy was later found dead.) Dr. Arthur Koehler, an expert on wood anatomy and identification at the Forest

Products Laboratory of the U.S. Forest Service, matched wood from a crude ladder left at the crime scene to a plank from the floor of the attic of Bruno Richard Hauptmann, the accused killer. Dr. Koehler testified about his findings during Hauptmann's trial. According to a story about the case at the Botanical Society of America's Web site, Dr. Koehler "presented three kinds of information from his study of the ladder: 1) identification of the wood used, 2) physical marks left by tools on the wood, and 3) comparisons of the wood structure."

Hauptmann's defense lawyer vigorously argued against allowing Dr. Koehler to testify. According to the transcript from the trial (*State of New Jersey v. Bruno Richard Hauptmann*), the defense lawyer argued "there is no such animal known among men as an expert on wood; that it is not a science that has been recognized by the courts; that it is not in a class with handwriting experts, with fingerprint experts, or with ballistic experts... The witness probably may testify as an experienced carpenter or something like that ... but when it comes to expressing an opinion as an expert or as a scientist, why that is quite different indeed. We say that the opinion of the jurors is just as good..." The judge responded, "I deam [sic] this witness to be qualified as an expert." This was the first time that forensic botany was accepted as testimony in an American court. Based on Dr. Koehler's findings and other evidence, Hauptmann was convicted and sentenced to death by electric chair.

Today, forensic botany is a small but growing forensic science specialty. The importance of gathering botanical evidence has even been mentioned in the FBI's *Handbook of Forensic Services*.

THE JOB

Forensic botanists draw on their knowledge of plant anatomy, structure, and environments to analyze plant samples found at crime scenes. It is the responsibility of forensic botanists to analyze the plant samples through various laboratory procedures and document their findings so they can be presented as evidence in legal proceedings. They use such laboratory equipment as microscopes to do so.

Plant material found at a crime scene can range from large pieces of wood or twigs; to plant leaves, petals, or stems that are visible to the naked eye; to much smaller—even microscopic—samples of spores, seeds, or pollen. This seemingly insignificant material may often times shed much light on what happened (or didn't happen) at the scene of a crime. In a murder investigation, for example, a suspect may inadvertently leave some plant samples at the scene of the crime that had adhered to their shoes or clothing. Using this material, forensic botanists can determine what plant the samples came from. If the plant is found only in certain locations, and not that of the crime scene, its presence may indicate where a suspect works or lives, or where the suspect was prior to the crime. Also, by comparing plant evidence found on a murder victim with the plant life present where the body was found, forensic botanists may determine if the victim was killed there, or if the body was likely moved to that location after the murder had been committed elsewhere. In an investigation where the remains of a body are discovered and investigators aren't sure how long ago the death occurred, forensic botanists can use their knowledge of growing seasons to help establish when the death occurred by analyzing any vegetation growing around the crime scene.

Forensic botanists spend the bulk of their time in the laboratory working with plant evidence collected from crime scenes. Because the evidence being analyzed is primarily intended to be used as evidence in a court of law, forensic botanists must take great care to carefully handle the samples, properly cataloging and storing the plant evidence throughout the process. They must take detailed notes about how and what was done to the evidence through the course of any tests or procedures, and prepare clear but thorough reports that document their findings. In addition to written notes and material, their documentation often includes photographs, illustrations, or video. Forensic botanists may be asked to testify in court regarding their findings or to explain the science involved so people without a background in botany can understand the relevance of the evidence.

REQUIREMENTS

High School

To prepare for a career in forensic botany, high school students can explore their interests by taking biology, doing science projects involving plants, and working during summers or school holidays for a nursery, park, or similar operation. College prep courses in chemistry, physics, biology, mathematics, English, and foreign language are a good idea because educational requirements for professional botanists are high. Additionally, take any forensic science or criminal justice classes that your school offers.

Postsecondary Training

Forensic botanists typically have at least a bachelor of science in botany or a related field. At the undergraduate level, there are numerous programs for degrees in botany or biology (which includes the study of botany). Many forensic botanists have graduate degrees or even doctorates in botany; many of these programs feature coursework in forensic botany. They also pursue postdoctoral positions in forensic botany to gain hands-on experience. Forensic botanists continue to learn throughout their careers by taking classes, workshops, and seminars, as well as reading professional journals and attending educational conferences.

Certification or Licensing

There is no specialized certification available for forensic botanists, but the American College of Forensic Examiners offers two certifications that may be helpful for workers in the field. The certified medical investigator program teaches forensic scientists how to correctly gather evidence at a crime scene and present it in court. The certified forensic consultant program provides an overview of the U.S. judicial system, and would be a good option for forensic botanists who are required to prepare interrogatories and deposition testimony and present oral testimony in court. Contact the college for more information.

Other Requirements

Forensic botanists enter the field because they want to combine their strong interests in plants with scientific study and research as they apply to criminal justice. As scientists, botanists need to be focused, patient, and determined. The ability to work on one's own is important, but few scientists work in a vacuum. They cooperate with others, share the results of their work orally and in writing, and, particularly in forensic botany, may need to explain what they're doing in layman's terms when they write reports and testify in court.

Educational requirements for botanists are high and so much of the work involves research. Therefore it is important to be a good scholar and enjoy digging for answers.

EXPLORING

The Botanical Society of America (BSA) suggests that high school students interested in general botany careers should take part in science fairs and clubs and get summer jobs with parks, nurseries, farms, experiment stations, labs, camps, florists, or landscape architects. Tour a botanical garden in your area and talk to staff. You can also get information by contacting national associations. For example, visit the Botanical Society of America's Web site (http://www.botany. org) to read a brochure on careers in botany. Although this brochure does not cover forensic botany, it will give you a general overview of the field. Books and magazines can provide general information on forensic science and the specialty of forensic botany.

EMPLOYERS

Forensic botanists are employed by crime labs, medical examiners' and coroners' offices, law enforcement agencies, lawyers, and any other organization or individual that needs plant evidence analyzed. Many forensic botanists work as freelance consultants. Botanists who work outside the field of forensic botany are employed by local, state, and federal agencies (including the Department of Agriculture; Environmental Protection Agency; Public Health Service; Biological Resources Discipline; and the National Aeronautics and Space Administration); colleges and universities; and in private industry, in agribusiness, biotechnology, biological supply, chemical botany, environmental botany, food, lumber and paper, pharmaceuticals, and petrochemicals. Botanists also work for greenhouses, arboretums, herbariums, seed and nursery companies, and fruit growers.

STARTING OUT

Very few, if any, botanists start their careers as forensic botanists. Instead, most enter the field as botanists in traditional fields and gradually develop their expertise by taking classes and pursuing other educational opportunities in forensic botany.

With a bachelor's degree, a botanist's first job may be as a technical assistant or technician for a lab. Those with a master's degree might get work on a university research project. Someone with a doctorate might get into research and development with a drug, pharmaceutical, or other manufacturer.

For some positions, contract work might be necessary before the botanist gains a full-time position. Contract work is work done on a per-project, or freelance, basis: You sign on for that one project, and then you move on. Contract workers are especially in demand in the summer when there's a lot of biology inventory work to be done.

College students typically learn about job openings from their professors or by accessing job leads through the school's career services office. The Internet is also a good place to seek out information on botany-related positions. Both the Botanical Society of America (http://www.botany.org) and the American Society of Plant Biologists (http://www.aspb.org) provide job listings at their Web sites.

ADVANCEMENT

Full-time forensic botanists who are employed by government agencies generally move up the ranks after gaining a certain number of hours of experience and obtaining advanced degrees or training. Botanists who work as consultants advance by receiving higher wages and working on higher-profile cases or for larger government agencies (such as the Federal Bureau of Investigation). The Botanical Society of America, whose membership primarily comes from universities, says keys for advancing in university positions include producing quality research, publishing a lot, and obtaining advanced degrees.

EARNINGS

There is no comprehensive information available regarding salaries for forensic botanists, but the U.S. Department of Labor (DoL) does provide salary data for soil and plant scientists (a category that includes botanists). According to the DoL, the median annual salary of soil and plant scientists was approximately $58,390 in 2008. The lowest paid 10 percent (which generally included those just starting out in the field) earned less than $34,260, while the highest paid 10 percent made approximately $105,340 or more per year. According to the National Association of Colleges and Employers, in 2007 graduates with a bachelor's degree in biological and life sciences received average starting salary offers of $34,953 a year. Soil and plant scientists working for the federal government earned mean salaries of $75,110 a year in 2008, and those employed at colleges and universities earned $50,840. Forensic botanists who have advanced training and experience can earn more than $110,000 annually.

Forensic botanists who work as consultants are typically paid by the hour or receive a flat fee based on the work assignment.

Benefits vary but usually include paid holidays and vacations, and health insurance. Self employed forensic botanists must provide their own benefits.

WORK ENVIRONMENT

Forensic botanists spend their days in a lab, poring over specimens and writing up the results of their research. They also occasionally travel to crime scenes to gather evidence. In the course of their work in the field, they may have to deal with adverse weather conditions (such as extremely hot weather or heavy rain) and grisly crime scenes.

OUTLOOK

Employment for all biological scientists, including botanists, is expected to grow about as fast as the average for all careers through 2016, according to the U.S. Department of Labor. Employment of forensic botanists will not be as strong. Only a small number of people work as forensic botanists, and most work part-time (while working full or part time as educators or botanists in other specialties). Despite this outlook, experts predict that this field will continue to grow as more law enforcement agencies become familiar with the work of forensic botanists and their role in solving crimes. Those with advanced education will have the best employment prospects.

FOR MORE INFORMATION

For information on forensic careers and education, contact
American Academy of Forensic Sciences
410 North 21st Street
Colorado Springs, CO 80904-2712
Tel: 719-636-1100
http://www.aafs.org

For information on forensic science and certification, contact
American College of Forensic Examiners
2750 East Sunshine Street
Springfield, MO 65804-2047
Tel: 800-423-9737
http://www.acfei.com

For information on careers in biology, contact
American Institute of Biological Sciences
1444 I Street, NW, Suite 200
Washington, DC 20005-6535
Tel: 202-628-1500
http://www.aibs.org

For general information about plant biology, contact
American Society of Plant Biologists
http://www.aspb.org

To read Careers in Botany *and* Botany for the Next Millennium, *visit the society's Web site.*
Botanical Society of America
PO Box 299
St. Louis, MO 63166-0299
Tel: 314-577-9566
Email: bsa-manager@botany.org
http://www.botany.org

Forensic Chemists

QUICK FACTS

School Subjects
Chemistry
Mathematics
Speech

Personal Skills
Technical/scientific

Work Environment
Primarily indoors
One location with some
travel

Minimum Education Level
Bachelor's degree

Salary Range
$37,840 to $66,230 to
$113,080+

Certification or Licensing
Voluntary

Outlook
About as fast as the average

DOT
022

GOE
02.02.01

NOC
2112

O*NET-SOC
19-2031.00

OVERVIEW

Chemists are scientists who study the composition, changes, reactions, and transformations of matter. They may specialize in analytical, biological, inorganic, organic, or physical chemistry. *Forensic chemists* are specialized chemists who conduct tests on evidence from crime scenes, such as paint chips, hair, fire debris, or glass fragments, either to identify unknown substances or to match the evidence against materials found on potential suspects. Approximately 83,000 chemists are employed in the United States. Only a small percentage of chemists specialize in forensic chemistry.

HISTORY

The ancient Egyptians, Greeks, and Romans were the first to use poisons. They were used both as a means of execution and murder. The Greek philosopher Socrates, for example, was sentenced to death by the state and forced to drink the poison hemlock. Arsenic was another popular poison. It was used because it was odorless and because it could easily be added to a person's food or drink. In 1752 a young woman in England named Mary Blandy used arsenic to poison her father, who died as a result of the poisoning. Blandy was tried for murder, and a physician named Anthony Addington developed a crude test for trace elements of arsenic that played a role in her conviction. This is considered the first test for a chemical poison in history. Various arsenic-detecting tests were developed in the following years, but it was not until 1836 that the chemist James Marsh developed the first test that could accurately detect the presence of arsenic in the

During testimony in court, a forensic chemist with the Massachusetts State Police holds up a knife found in an accused murderer's apartment. *(Michael Dwyer, AP Photo)*

body. Shortly thereafter, Christian Friedrich Samuel Hahnemann, the German physician and founder of homeopathy, created an even more accurate test that is still used in some circumstances today.

The emergence of tests for the presence of poisons, blood, semen, hair, and other substances have helped law enforcement officials apprehend criminals and convict them in court. Forensic chemists are important members of the criminal justice team—especially with the emergence of DNA analysis technology and other high-tech scientific methods to collect and study evidence.

THE JOB

Forensic chemists study a variety of evidence from many different types of cases. They may perform blood-typing and other tests on body fluids such as saliva, blood, or semen in cases involving sexual assault or disputed paternity. They analyze evidence from fires and compare it to known accelerants such as gasoline in an effort to determine if a fire was set deliberately. They can identify the unique properties of fingerprints or gunpowder residue from firearms. They also perform chemical analysis of new compounds, including alternative fuels such as biodiesel, for possible future use in matching against crime-scene evidence. Forensic chemists also play a major role in the fight against trafficking of illegal drugs; they work to identify new substances that appear on the market, and they may also be called in to assist in the dangerous task of cleaning up illegal drug labs. These specialists are often known as *forensic drug chemists* or *forensic drug analysts*.

Forensic chemists use a wide range of analytic techniques and the latest in high-tech instruments, including ultraviolet and infrared spectrophotometry and high-pressure liquid chromatography.

Forensic chemists may be asked to testify in court regarding their findings. As a result, it is extremely important that they are skilled at conducting accurate investigations, handling evidence properly, and writing detailed reports about their findings.

Forensic chemists must be willing to continue learning about their field throughout their careers. Some write articles about the field, which are published in technical journals or presented to other chemists at educational conferences. The sharing of information with others in the field strengthens the abilities of forensic chemists worldwide and aids in the development of new research methods; for example, a forensic chemist with the Bureau of Alcohol, Tobacco, Firearms and Explosives who specializes in fire investigation used his experience in the field to expand and increase the efficiency of the bureau's fire-accelerant canine detection unit.

Although most forensic chemists are civilian workers, some are sworn law enforcement officers.

REQUIREMENTS

High School

If you are interested in a career in forensic chemistry, begin preparing yourself in high school by taking advanced-level courses in the physical sciences, mathematics, and English. A year each of physics, chemistry, and biology is essential, as are the abilities to read graphs and charts, perform difficult mathematical calculations, and write scientific reports. Computer science courses are also important to take, since much of your documentation and other work will involve using computers. Taking speech classes will help you to communicate effectively with your coworkers and testify in court.

Postsecondary Training

The minimum educational requirement for a chemist is a bachelor's degree in chemistry, forensic science, or a related field. An emphasis on analytical chemistry is preferred by employers. However, in the upper levels of basic and applied research, and especially in a university setting, most positions are filled by people with doctoral degrees.

More than 640 bachelor's, 310 master's, and 200 doctoral degree programs are accredited by the American Chemical Society (ACS). Many colleges and universities also offer advanced degree programs in chemistry. Upon entering college, students majoring in chemistry must expect to take classes in several branches of the field, such as organic, inorganic, analytical, physical chemistry, and biochemistry. Chemistry majors must advance their skills in mathematics, physics, and biology, and be proficient with computers.

Beyond the obviously necessary background in chemistry and instrumental analysis, it is helpful for forensic chemists to have some knowledge of biology, geology, and soil chemistry, among others. There has recently been a greater emphasis placed on the study of genetics as the use and analysis of DNA evidence has increased.

The American Academy of Forensic Sciences offers a list of colleges and universities that offer degrees in forensic chemistry or related fields at its Web site, http://www.aafs.org.

Once hired, forensic chemists receive on-the-job training both in laboratory and classroom settings. They also continue to upgrade their skills throughout their careers by participating in seminars, workshops, and conferences—many of which are offered by professional associations.

Certification or Licensing

The International Association for Identification offers several certification categories that may be of interest to forensic chemists, including certified crime scene analyst and bloodstain pattern examiner certification. Contact the association for more information.

The American College of Forensic Examiners offers the certified forensic consultant program, which provides an overview of the U.S. judicial system. This certification would be useful for forensic chemists who are required to testify in court. Contact the college for more information.

Other Requirements

Forensic chemists must be detail-oriented, precise workers. They often work with minute quantities, taking minute measurements. They must record all details and reaction changes that may seem insignificant and unimportant to the untrained observer. They must keep careful records of their work and have the patience to repeat experiments or tests over and over again. They should be inquisitive and have an interest in what makes things work and how pieces of evidence fit together. Forensic chemists may work alone or in groups. A successful forensic chemist is not only self-motivated but should be a team player.

Public-speaking skills are important for forensic chemists, who are often summoned to court to testify about and explain their findings. Some employers of forensic chemists may even put their new hires through several months of practice in courtroom testimony in addition to their regular training. Integrity and the ability to remain impartial are important qualities; the forensic chemist must not let his or her conclusions be influenced by parties on either side of a court case.

EXPLORING

The best means of exploring a career in chemistry while still in high school is to pay attention and work hard in chemistry class. This will give you the opportunity to learn the scientific method, perform chemical experiments, and become familiar with chemical terminology. Contact departments of chemistry at local colleges or universities to discuss the field and arrange tours of their laboratories or classrooms. Due to the extensive training involved, it is very unlikely that a high school student will be able to get a summer job or internship working in a laboratory. However, you may want to contact local manufacturers or research institutions to explore the possibility.

If you are interested in a career in forensic chemistry, ask your science teacher or school counselor to arrange an information interview with a forensic chemist or set up a tour of a forensic laboratory. Reading books about the field will provide you with useful information. Here is one suggestion: *Crime Scene Chemistry for the Armchair Sleuth,* by Cathy Cobb, Monty L. Fetterolf, and Jack G. Goldsmith. You might also try to attend a trial where a forensic chemist is testifying.

EMPLOYERS

Approximately 83,000 chemists are employed in the United States, with only a small percentage specializing in forensic chemistry. Forensic chemists spend the majority of their working hours in laboratories associated with federal, state, or local police departments, medical examiner's offices, or other government agencies such as the Federal Bureau of Investigation. There are also some private companies that perform forensic analysis. Other forensic chemists work as teachers at colleges and universities.

Chemists who do not specialize in forensic chemistry work for manufacturing companies, government agencies (such as the Department of Health and Human Services, the Department of Agriculture, the Department of Energy, and the National Institute of Standards and Technology), in laboratories at institutions of higher learning that are devoted to research, and in full-time teaching positions at high schools and universities.

STARTING OUT

Once you have a degree in chemistry or forensic chemistry, job opportunities will begin to become available. Summer jobs may become available after your sophomore or junior year of college. You can attend career fairs to meet and perhaps interview prospective employers. Professors or faculty advisers may know of job openings, and you can begin breaking into the field by using these connections. Your college's career services office will also have a listing of available jobs in the field.

If you are a senior and are interested in pursuing an academic career at a college or university, you should apply to graduate schools. You will want to begin focusing even more on the specific type of chemistry you wish to practice and teach (for example, analytical chemistry or forensic chemistry if you want to become a forensic chemist). Look for universities that have strong programs and eminent professors in your intended field of specialty. By getting involved with the basic research of a specific branch of chemistry while in graduate school, you can become a highly employable expert in your field.

ADVANCEMENT

In nonacademic careers, advancement usually takes the form of increased job responsibilities accompanied by salary increases. For example, a forensic chemist may rise from doing basic research in a laboratory to being a group leader, overseeing and directing the work of others. Some forensic chemists eventually leave the laboratory and set up their own consulting businesses, serving the needs of private labs or government agencies. Others may accept university faculty positions.

Forensic chemists who work in a university setting follow the advancement procedures for that institution. Typically, a forensic chemist in academia with a doctoral degree will go from instructor to assistant professor to associate professor and finally to full professor. In order to advance through these ranks, faculty members at most colleges and universities are expected to perform original research and publish their papers in scientific journals of chemistry, forensic chemistry, and/or other sciences. As the rank of faculty members increases, so do their duties, salaries, responsibilities, and reputations.

There are also a number of related options for the forensic chemist to keep in mind, such as teaching or administrative work. For example, the director of a crime lab may move up from doing day-to-day analysis to become a supervisor of other forensic scientists. Some forensic chemists use what they have learned to enter the fields of pharmaceutical drug development or patent law.

EARNINGS

There is no comprehensive salary information available for forensic chemists, but the U.S. Department of Labor (DoL) provides information on earnings for all chemists regardless of practice area. According to the DoL, median annual earnings for all chemists in 2008 were $66,230. The lowest paid 10 percent earned less than $37,840, and the highest paid 10 percent made more than $113,080 annually. Chemists working for the federal government had mean annual incomes of $98,060 in 2008. Salary levels for chemists vary based on education, experience, and the area in which they work.

As highly trained, full-time professionals, most forensic chemists receive health insurance, paid vacations, and sick leave. The specifics of these benefits vary from employer to employer. Forensic chemists who teach at the college or university level usually work on an academic calendar, which means they get extensive breaks from teaching classes during summer and winter recesses.

WORK ENVIRONMENT

Most forensic chemists work in clean, well-lighted laboratories that are organized and neatly kept, although government labs can sometimes be small, underfunded, and understaffed. They may have their own offices and share laboratory space with other forensic chemists. Occasionally, chemical reactions or substances being tested may have strong odors. Other chemicals may be extremely dangerous to the touch, and forensic chemists will have to wear protective devices such as goggles, gloves, and protective clothing and work in special, well-ventilated hoods.

Some forensic chemists are required to testify in criminal cases, which can involve stressful situations when their testimony is questioned by defense attorneys.

OUTLOOK

The U.S. Department of Labor predicts that employment for chemists will grow about as fast as the average for all careers through 2016. Opportunities should also be good for forensic chemists. The growth in the use of DNA evidence and profiling is expected to create more jobs for forensic chemists. Aspiring forensic chemists will do well to earn doctoral degrees to maximize their opportunities for employment and advancement.

Those wishing to teach full-time at the university or college level should find opportunities but also stiff competition. Many of these institutions are choosing to hire people for adjunct faculty positions (part-time positions without benefits) instead of for full-time, tenure-track positions. Nevertheless, well-trained forensic chemists should have little trouble finding some type of employment.

FOR MORE INFORMATION

For information on forensic careers and education, contact
American Academy of Forensic Sciences
410 North 21st Street
Colorado Springs, CO 80904-2712
Tel: 719-636-1100
http://www.aafs.org

For information about clinical laboratory careers, contact
American Association for Clinical Chemistry
1850 K Street, NW, Suite 625
Washington, DC 20006-2215
Tel: 800-892-1400
http://www.aacc.org

For information about forensic chemistry careers and approved general education chemistry programs, contact
American Chemical Society
1155 16th Street, NW
Washington, DC 20036-4839
Tel: 800-227-5558
http://www.chemistry.org

The council offers information about the chemical industry and the use of chemistry in the field of forensic science, and maintains an informative Web site.
American Chemistry Council
1300 Wilson Boulevard

Arlington VA 22209-2323
Tel: 703-741-5000
http://www.americanchemistry.com

For information on forensic science and certification, contact
American College of Forensic Examiners
2750 East Sunshine Street
Springfield, MO 65804-2047
Tel: 800-423-9737
http://www.acfei.com

To learn more about forensic services at the FBI, visit the FBI Laboratory Division's Web site.
Federal Bureau of Investigation (FBI)
J. Edgar Hoover Building
935 Pennsylvania Avenue, NW
Washington, DC 20535-0001
Tel: 202-324-3000
http://www.fbi.gov/hq/lab/labhome.htm

For information on certification, contact
International Association for Identification
2535 Pilot Knob Road, Suite 117
Mendota Heights, MN 55120-1120
Tel: 651-681-8566
http://www.theiai.org

INTERVIEW

Louis Maucieri is a forensic training consultant in Sacramento, California. He discussed his career and the field of forensic science with the editors of Careers in Focus: Forensics.

Q. What made you want to enter this career?
A. Before beginning a career in forensics, I applied my chemistry degree working nine years in the fuels and propellant industries. I wanted a job change and took a qualifying exam. Using my training and experience to assist law enforcement was a major reason for entering a forensic career path.

Q. What are some of the pros and cons of work in the field?
A. [A positive aspect of this career is that] it's a profession with independence of opinion. Each case is unique. Evidence sam-

ples are always challenging. You work in crime scenes, labs, and courts. Negative factors are that opportunities for public-funded labs are limited by fiscal problems. Working in a small two- to five-person lab will offer far less opportunities for training and advancement.

Q. What is the future employment outlook for forensic science?

A. Future employment outlook is always budget driven—city, county, state, and federal level. Presently the job picture is following the economic downturn nationally. Opportunities in private labs can follow growth in population and crime generally. At this writing, there are studies to fund a national initiative to have all criminal cases reworked by a second lab. This would at least double the need for forensic scientists.

Q. What have been some of your most rewarding or interesting experiences in the field?

A. In my 30 years, five months, and 29 days at a forensic career, I had some notable cases. One was the "San Quentin Six" jail break and multiple murders. The ringleader smuggled a 9 mm pistol under his wig back into the compound. He released all the Black Panther inmates kept in the "Adjustment center" and, running into the yard, was shot by tower guards. Walking through the crime scene meant stepping through and around quarter-inch thick pools of blood. Lab analysis included fingerprints, many bloodstains, smuggled chemicals, fired bullets, and zip guns. The first trial was in 1975—five days on the stand with six lawyers. The six defendants were chained to the courtroom floor with cuffs on their wrists.

Another was a crime scene I did at a ranch owned by the Hells Angels. They had dumped three (at least) murder victims in three-foot-wide well casings on the property. They poured lime (CaO) on the bodies, thinking it was lye that would dissolve their victims. The lime preserved them and, starting with a back-hoe, I recovered three bodies from ~12-foot depths. Autopsies by pathologist, dental X rays, and lab analysis followed. Trial was [about] three years later.

The case where I learned the most was the "tracer bullet" case. Some hunters had fired tracer rounds into a mountain, starting a wildlands fire. Air tankers were called in, and one of them crashed, killing the pilot. After two weeks, investigators recovered two battered tracer bullets by sifting the dirt at the point of origin. I test fired six .30 caliber rifles, for comparison to the tracers—but we could not match them to the battered slugs. But one rifle had orange paint in the barrel breech. I matched this to the orange paint on the recovered 7.62 mm NATO tracer ammunition in the suspect jeep. Comparison included color by microscopy, and instrumental analysis of bullet tip paint and pyrotechnic ash in the fired bullets.

Twice I was assigned as supervising criminalist. I assigned cases and reviewed staff reports for accuracy. I testified in 33 counties of California [on about] 18 different evidence types. In 2008 I testified [regarding] a 1982 crime scene I did in a homicide case.

I was assigned to help write the enabling legislation for the California Criminalistics Institute (CCI)—a training and research lab for all 35 city, county, state labs in California. As the first technical staff hired, I was responsible for the Quality Assurance Program for 14 state forensic field labs. I manufactured and tracked more than 400 various proficiency tests for ~ 150 staff. I also provided special training classes in case review, quality assurance, and courtroom testimony. CCI called me back from retirement to continue giving training to forensic staff. I also teach a graduate school class on scientific evidence and courtroom testimony at the University of California-Davis.

Forensic Engineers

OVERVIEW

Engineers are problem-solvers who use the principles of mathematics and science to plan, design, and create ways to make things work better. Engineers are needed in every field imaginable. In fact, more than 25 engineering disciplines are recognized by professional engineering societies. *Forensic engineers* are specialized engineers who study materials, devices, structures, and products that do not work as they were designed or fail to work completely. They have backgrounds in many different engineering disciplines. There are approximately 1.5 million engineers employed in the United States; only a small percentage of this number are forensic engineers.

HISTORY

Building has been one of humanity's basic activities. The development of civilization is marked by the building of pyramids, bridges, roadways, temples, aqueducts, walls and fortifications, canals, and many other structures. These projects were designed and supervised by the earliest form of civil engineers. These engineers had to design methods of moving large and cumbersome stones for buildings, sometimes across a long distance. To accomplish this without the benefit of motorized vehicles, early engineers designed rollers, pulleys, levers, and hydraulics. The understanding of force and counterforce allowed the engineers to design ways to decrease the physical

QUICK FACTS

School Subjects
Mathematics
Physics

Personal Skills
Leadership/management
Technical/scientific

Work Environment
Indoors and outdoors
Primarily multiple locations

Minimum Education Level
Bachelor's degree

Salary Range
$49,270 to $88,570 to
$132,070+

Certification or Licensing
Voluntary (certification)
Required for certain
positions (licensing)

Outlook
About as fast as the average

DOT
003, 005, 007, 008, 010,
012, 013, 014, 015, 019,
024, 638, 950, 953

GOE
05.01.01, 05.01.03,
05.01.04, 05.01.06,
05.01.07, 05.01.08

NOC
2122, 2131, 2132, 2133,
2134, 2141, 2142, 2143,
2144, 2145, 2147, 2148,
2173, 4121

(continues)

QUICK FACTS

(continued)

O*NET-SOC
17-2011.00, 17-2021.00,
17-2031.00, 17-2041.00,
17-2051.00, 17-2061.00,
17-2071.00, 17-2072.00,
17-2081.00, 17-2111.01,
17-2111.02, 17-2111.03,
17-2112.00, 17-2121.01,
17-2121.02, 17-2131.00,
17-2141.00, 17-2151.00,
17-2161.00, 17-2171.00,
17-2199.00

effort needed by the builders to move massive stones. Without this, structures like the pyramids would not have been possible.

Engineers have influenced discoveries and inventions more than workers in any other profession. The work of engineers has a more thorough impact on all human life than any other discipline. But despite this expertise, sometimes products, machinery, tools, and other manufactured items fail to work as designed—others fail completely, causing loss of life and personal injury. One of the earliest examples of the work of forensic engineers during modern times occurred after the collapse of the Dee Bridge in Chester, England, on May 24, 1847. A passenger fell through the bridge, killing five people. An accident inquiry by the Royal Engineers, a branch of the British army, found that the architect's design was flawed. After this accident, and the resulting inquiry, architects and builders became more cognizant of the importance of careful planning and the use of established engineering principles when designing a project.

Today, forensic engineers work in nearly every engineering discipline—investigating everything from faulty engine parts on automobiles to major disasters such as bridge and building collapses; airplane, automobile, and train crashes and collisions; and nearly any other part, product, mechanism, system, or structure that does not perform up to expectations.

THE JOB

Forensic engineers investigate materials, products, structures or components that fail or do not operate or function as intended; these defects or failures often cause damage to property, injury, or even death. Their reports and judgments about the causes of failure are used as evidence in personal-injury lawsuits, contract or warranty disputes, and patent and copyright infringement litigation, in addition to criminal cases. In recent years, forensic engineers have played a key role investigating some of the major accidents and terrorist acts in recent history—ranging from both space shuttle disasters; to engineering studies conducted to determine why both towers of the

World Trade Center collapsed so quickly on September 11, 2001; to the I-35W Bridge collapse in Minnesota.

Forensic engineers are often called in to help determine what caused a building collapse, a train or plane crash, or even a car accident, particularly if some component of the machinery involved is suspected of having failed. They interview witnesses or, ideally, persons who were operating the suspected faulty machinery, and they often reconstruct the accident scene to get a better idea of what happened. They examine machine parts that have failed. They use microscopes and magnifying glasses to determine whether corrosion, fatigue, sabotage, or some other factor was the reason for the failure. Accidents involving fire are especially challenging, since critical evidence is often destroyed, but in many instances the forensic engineer can shed light on whether a gas leak, an electrical problem, a cooking accident, or even arson may have been the cause.

Manufacturers of appliances, consumer products, medical devices, and even hand tools use the talents of forensic engineers to locate possible causes of failure in their products. Many defects in these items are eliminated through testing in the factory before the product is placed on the market, but if some unforeseen failure comes to light, particularly one that can place the user of the product in danger, the product may be recalled or even completely withdrawn from the market and the forensic engineer will be asked to answer, as quickly as possible, the question, "What happened?" Examples of this include artificial hearts, heart valves, breast implants, brake systems, airbags, and power drills.

One of the most popular specialties for forensic engineers is traffic accident investigation. *Traffic accident investigators* analyze the cause and circumstances of traffic accidents, usually when an accident is suspected to be the result of negligence.

Traffic accident investigators try to determine the cause of traffic accidents. They examine the circumstances of an accident in order to determine why it occurred, using any physical evidence from the accident, testimony of people who witnessed the accident, reports prepared by law enforcement officials, and other types documentation, such as diagrams, photographs, and video recordings of the accident scene. In their analysis, accident investigators take into account such factors as the weather (Was it clear, rainy, or foggy at the time of the accident?), time of day (Did the accident occur during daylight hours, or when it was dark?), and physical condition of the street and surrounding area (Was the street relatively smooth, or was it filled with potholes? Or was it a poorly maintained gravel road? Was the surface slippery due to ice, rain, or the presence of a foreign substance? Was it well-lit, or dark and shadowy?). Then they take into consideration variables such as any known or potential equipment malfunctions (such as faulty brakes on one of the vehicles, or malfunctioning gates at a railroad crossing), the speed of the vehicle(s) involved in the accident, the severity of impact, and the damage or injuries that occurred as a result of the accident. Using these types of materials and knowledge, accident investigators analyze what happened. Often times they physically reconstruct the accident in order to gain a better idea of what occurred; to do this, they typically obtain like or similar vehicles and recreate the circumstances of the accident.

When traffic accident investigators are finished with their investigations, they compile thorough reports that include their findings and the conclusions they have drawn from their analysis. Perhaps a crash between two vehicles was the result of a faulty traffic signal, or because one of the vehicles hit a patch of ice on the road. Or maybe the driver of one of the vehicles was intoxicated and did not stop in time when the traffic light turned red at a busy intersection.

All forensic engineers must be very careful and detailed in carrying out their investigations and with creating their reports, which are frequently used as evidence in legal proceedings—both in civil litigation and in criminal cases. Their work can also be utilized outside of the legal system; for example, insurance companies rely on the skills of forensic engineers in settling insurance claims. To help others understand their analysis of an accident, forensic engineers may provide more than just a written account of what happened and the conclusions they've reached; a written report might be supplemented by illustrations, models, or computer animations. Forensic engineers are often asked to testify in court to explain their findings.

Engineers are assisted by *engineering technicians* and *technologists*. These workers are employed in all engineering disciplines, and are differentiated most commonly by the type of education they receive. Engineering technicians typically have an associate degree in engineering technology, although some learn their skills via a combination of postsecondary training and on-the-job training. Engineering technologists typically have a bachelor's degree in engineering technology. Some engineering technicians and technologists pursue advanced education and become engineers.

REQUIREMENTS

High School

High school students interested in forensic engineering should take a great deal of mathematics, including geometry, trigonometry, calculus, and two years of algebra. They should develop a strong background in physics, chemistry, biology, and computer programming or applications. Because forensic engineers must communicate constantly with other engineers, scientists, clients, and consumers, four years of language arts are essential.

Postsecondary Training
Only a few colleges and universities offer courses in forensic engineering. Forensic engineers typically earn a minimum of a bachelor's degree in engineering or an allied science and develop their own credentials via on-the-job experience and by taking continuing education classes, seminars, and workshops that are applicable to their specialty in the field, such as vehicle accident investigation. Most forensic engineers have a master's degree or doctorate in their chosen discipline, such as mechanical, environmental, or aerospace engineering. The Accreditation Board for Engineering and Technology offers a list of accredited postsecondary engineering programs at its Web site or (http://www.abet.org).

Certification or Licensing
Many engineers become certified. Certification is a status granted by a technical or professional organization for the purpose of recognizing and documenting an individual's abilities in a specific engineering field.

Licensure as a professional engineer is recommended since an increasing number of employers require it. Even those employers who do not require licensing will view it favorably when considering new hires or when reviewing workers for promotion. Licensing requirements vary from state to state. In general, however, they involve having graduated from an accredited school, having four years of work experience, and having passed the eight-hour Fundamentals of Engineering exam and the eight-hour Principles and Practice of Engineering exam. Depending on your state, you can take the Fundamentals exam shortly before your graduation from college or after you have received your bachelor's degree. At that point you will be an engineer-in-training (EIT). Once you have fulfilled all the licensure requirements, you receive the designation professional engineer (PE). Visit the National Council of Examiners for Engineering and Surveying's Web site (http://www.ncees.org) for more information on licensure.

Other Requirements
In addition to the math and science background necessary for any career in engineering, forensic engineers should be creative, inquisitive, analytical, and detail oriented and possess good "detective"

skills. Especially in accident cases, they need to be aware that factors other than mechanical failure may be involved. The Chernobyl nuclear disaster in the Soviet Union in 1986, for example, is often cited as an example of the dangers of nuclear power, when in fact the accident was caused by human error. Forensic engineers should also enjoy solving problems and developing logical plans. They often work on projects in multidisciplinary teams, so prospective engineers should be able to work well both alone and with others. Finally, forensic engineers must be able to describe their work and their findings in a clear manner in courts of law and be prepared to withstand attacks on their methods and credentials by attorneys on the other side of the aisle.

EXPLORING

Perhaps the best way for high school students to explore the field of engineering is by contacting the Junior Engineering Technical Society (JETS). JETS can help you learn about different fields within engineering (including forensic engineering) and can guide you toward science and engineering fairs.

Participation in science and engineering fairs can be an invaluable experience for a high school student interested in engineering. Through these fairs, you learn to do your own research and applications in an engineering field. Too often, students leave high school with a strong academic background in mathematics and sciences, but have never applied their knowledge to the real world. By developing a project for a fair, you begin to learn how to think like an engineer by creatively using your academic knowledge to solve real-life problems.

You can also visit the Web sites of general engineering professional associations, as well as those that specialize in forensic engineering. One interesting site is the Component Failure Museum (http://materials.open.ac.uk/mem/index.htm), which provides descriptions and photographs that detail why tools, parts, and building materials failed to perform as designed. Reading books and periodicals about forensic engineering and engineering in general will also provide you with a good introduction to the work of engineers.

EMPLOYERS

Approximately 1.5 million engineers are employed in the United States, but only a very small number of engineers specialize in forensic engineering. Engineers may classify themselves as aeronautical, aerospace, electrical, industrial, or mechanical engineers and also provide forensic engineering-related consulting services. Forensic engineers work for large corporations, small engineering firms, independent consultants, insurance companies, law firms, and local, state, and federal government agencies. Some federal employers of engineers include the National Aeronautics and Space Administration, and the Departments of Agriculture, Defense, Energy, Homeland Security, and Transportation. Other possibilities for engineers can be found in academia as instructors or researchers or as writers for engineering-oriented publications. Many forensic engineers are self-employed. They work part time as forensic engineering consultants and the remainder of the time as educators or as engineers in traditional engineering disciplines, such as mechanical engineering.

STARTING OUT

No one starts out in their career as a forensic engineer. Instead they begin as traditional engineers in their chosen discipline and gain job skills and experience that will eventually allow them to advertise their services as forensic engineers.

College and graduate school programs can help newly degreed engineers locate jobs. These schools are often in touch with prospective employers who are in need of engineers. Conferences, trade shows, and engineering career fairs can also be good places for new engineers to begin meeting employers and setting up interviews. The American Association of Engineering Societies maintains a membership list of the various engineering societies of each field. College graduates can contact these societies to find out about gaining employment in the field, calendars of events such as conferences or fairs, and more.

ADVANCEMENT

As forensic engineers gain more experience they are given greater responsibilities and tougher problems to solve. At this stage, the engineer will be involved in more decision making and independent work. Some engineers advance to become engineering team managers or supervisors of entire projects. They also may enter administrative positions. In addition, many high level corporate and government executives started out as engineers.

Advancement depends upon experience and education. The more experience forensic engineers get, the more independence and responsibilities they will probably gain; however, an engineer with a bachelor's degree will, in all probability, not make it to the highest levels of the field. Engineers who are interested in going into corporate, industrial, or executive positions often go back to school to earn degrees in law or business.

EARNINGS

Engineers earn some of the highest starting salaries of any career. The U.S. Department of Labor does not provide salary information for the specialization of forensic engineer, but it does provide salary data for engineers not otherwise categorized. Salaries for these engineers ranged from less than $49,270 to $132,070 or more in 2008. The median salary was $88,570. Forensic engineers who work as consultants typically charge by the hour. Experienced engineers may charge clients anywhere from $100 to $325 an hour, plus expenses.

Full-time forensic engineers usually receive benefits such as vacation days, sick leave, health and life insurance, and a savings and pension program. Self-employed engineers must provide their own benefits.

WORK ENVIRONMENT

Engineers usually have a central office from which they base their work, and these offices are typically quite pleasant, clean, and climate-controlled. Engineers often have clerical, research, and technical staffs working for them at these offices.

Most engineers, however, are required to spend at least part of their time on a specific work site, and these sites may be noisy, dusty, dirty, and unpleasant. They often travel to disaster or accident sites to gather information and interview witnesses. People interested in becoming engineers should be flexible about work sites and adjust easily to different types of environments.

While it is fun to solve problems and develop innovations, engineering is a serious job. People rely on engineers in some way for their safety and well-being. They want to be sure that their houses and offices are sturdy, their cars safe, and their food is processed and packaged safely. Because technology has become so omnipresent in society, people have become accustomed to trusting engineers with their safety. A good engineer must work to be deserving of this trust.

OUTLOOK

Employment for engineers is expected to grow about as fast as the average for all occupations through 2016, according to the U.S. Department of Labor. Steady employment for forensic engineers is also expected because workers with this type of specialized technical expertise are in short supply.

Engineers have traditionally enjoyed great employment security because their work is so essential to maintaining and advancing America's infrastructure and industry. Even in times of economic decline, engineers' jobs are generally safe. Engineers who stay current concerning the latest technologies and remain flexible in regards to type of employer, location, and other factors will most likely ensure themselves of employment for years to come.

FOR MORE INFORMATION

For a list of accredited college engineering programs, contact
Accreditation Board for Engineering and Technology
111 Market Place, Suite 1050
Baltimore, MD 21202-7116
Tel: 410-347-7700
http://www.abet.org

For information on certification, careers, and salaries or a copy of Environmental Engineering Selection Guide *(which lists names of accredited environmental engineering programs), contact*
American Academy of Environmental Engineers
130 Holiday Court, Suite 100
Annapolis, MD 21401-7003
Tel: 410-266-3311
Email: info@aaee.net
http://www.aaee.net

For information on forensic careers, education, and its membership section for forensic engineers, contact
American Academy of Forensic Sciences
410 North 21st Street
Colorado Springs, CO 80904-2712
Tel: 719-636-1100
http://www.aafs.org

For information on certification, contact
American College of Forensic Examiners
2750 East Sunshine Street
Springfield, MO 65804-2047
Tel: 800-423-9737
http://www.acfei.com

For career information and details on student branches of this organization, contact
American Institute of Aeronautics and Astronautics
1801 Alexander Bell Drive, Suite 500
Reston, VA 20191-4344
Tel: 800-639-2422
http://www.aiaa.org

For information on career opportunities, contact
American Institute of Chemical Engineers
3 Park Avenue
New York, NY 10016-5991
Tel: 800-242-4363
http://www.aiche.org

For more information on careers in engineering, contact
American Society for Engineering Education
1818 N Street, NW, Suite 600
Washington, DC 20036-2479
Tel: 202-331-3500
http://www.asee.org

For information on careers and scholarships, contact
American Society of Civil Engineers
1801 Alexander Bell Drive
Reston, VA 20191-4400
Tel: 800-548-2723
http://www.asce.org

For information on mechanical engineering and mechanical engineering technology, contact
ASME International
Three Park Avenue
New York, NY 10016-5990
Tel: 800-843-2763
Email: infocentral@asme.org
http://www.asme.org

For information on careers and educational programs, contact
Institute of Electrical and Electronics Engineers
2001 L Street, NW, Suite 700
Washington, DC 20036-4910

Tel: 202-785-0017
Email: ieeeusa@ieee.org
http://www.ieee.org

For comprehensive information about careers in industrial engineering, contact
Institute of Industrial Engineers
3577 Parkway Lane, Suite 200
Norcross, GA 30092-2833
Tel: 800-494-0460
http://www.iienet.org

For information on careers, contact
Institute of Transportation Engineers
1099 14th Street, NW, Suite 300 West
Washington, DC 20005-3438
Tel: 202-289-0222
Email: ite_staff@ite.org
http://www.ite.org

For information on careers in forensic engineering and other engineering specialties and student clubs and competitions, contact
Junior Engineering Technical Society
1420 King Street, Suite 405
Alexandria, VA 22314-2794
Tel: 703-548-5387
Email: info@jets.org
http://www.jets.org

For general information about forensic engineering, contact
National Academy of Forensic Engineers
174 Brady Avenue
Hawthorne, NY 10532-2207
Tel: 866-NAFEORG
http://www.nafe.org

For information on licensure and practice areas, contact
National Society of Professional Engineers
1420 King Street
Alexandria, VA 22314-2794
Tel: 703-684-2800
http://www.nspe.org

For information on automotive engineering, contact
SAE International
400 Commonwealth Drive
Warrendale, PA 15096-0001
Tel: 877-606-7323
http://www.sae.org

For industry information, contact
Society of Forensic Engineers and Scientists
Email: info@forensic-society.org
http://forensic-society.org

For information about manufacturing engineering, contact
Society of Manufacturing Engineers
One SME Drive
Dearborn, MI 48121-2408
Tel: 800-733-4763
http://www.sme.org

Forensic Entomologists

OVERVIEW

Entomologists study insects and their relationship to other life forms. *Forensic entomologists* are specialized entomologists who use insect-related evidence and their knowledge of insects to provide facts for civil and criminal cases. They are sometimes referred to as *medical entomologists* or *medicocriminal entomologists* in criminal investigations.

HISTORY

In the past, the maggots and other insects crawling in the eyes, nose, and wounds on dead bodies were long considered a disgusting part of the decay process, and were largely avoided by forensic investigators. They instead typically concentrated on such things as fingerprints, gunpowder residue, ballistics, and blood spatters. Through the years, however, a few scientists have researched the clues insects provide and in the last 25 years, entomology has become an important part of forensic science. But the principles of forensic entomology have been observed or in use for centuries.

One of the first recorded cases that demonstrated the principles of what would later be known as forensic entomology was in the 13th century, when Song Ci (also known as Sung Tz'u) documented a death investigation in a Chinese village. The weapon that caused the death was determined to be a sickle, a very common tool in the village. Since no one claimed to have any knowledge of the death, the sickle of every villager was examined.

Only one attracted flies, due to the traces of human tissue that still remained on it. The owner of that sickle subsequently confessed to murdering the victim. The findings of Song Ci, including more detailed analyses of insects found on the dead body, were published in *The Washing Away of Wrongs* in 1247.

A noteworthy experiment that also demonstrated forensic entomological principles was conducted in 1668 by Francesco L. Redi, an Italian doctor. Redi studied the decomposition of meat, some of which was protected from insect infestation, and some that was exposed to insects. The first known instance of insects being used to determine the age of human remains occurred in 1855, when Bergeret d'Arbois, a French doctor, used entomological principles to determine the time of death of the remains of a child that was discovered behind a mantle in a house. This was important because the people who currently lived in the house were under suspicion for the child's murder, but Bergeret was able to determine that the death of the child occurred long before they moved into the home. Later that century, another Frenchman by the name of Jean Pierre Megnin documented forensic entomological principles when he published *La Faune des Cadavres* in 1894. Megnin was a veterinarian, and his book was the result of many years of study and provided information on insects that could be used in death investigations.

Advances in the study of forensic entomology continued in the 20th century as entomological knowledge expanded and technological advances provided for new methods of study and investigation. Today, forensic entomology can play a vital role in civil and criminal investigations.

THE JOB

Forensic entomologists use their knowledge of insects—such as where they live, their life cycle, and their behaviors—to interpret evidence in legal matters. In a criminal case, for example, a forensic entomologist can often determine the general time, location, and even the likely cause of death by using insect evidence gathered from and around a murder victim. In a civil case forensic entomologists might be called on to use their skills to determine when and where an insect infestation began and how far it has progressed, useful in cases where someone is trying to determine who is responsible for the problem and therefore liable for any damaged incurred.

Forensic entomologists may work in the field collecting evidence; those involved in murder cases may also do some collection and observation at the morgue and during the autopsy. They use different tools to collect the evidence; delicate larvae and eggs might be collected with a paintbrush, whereas larger insects might be collected with forceps. Different types of insects and insects in various stages of their life cycles must be stored separately when collected from the field. Usually some of the samples of each type of insect-related evidence are immediately preserved in alcohol, while the remainder of each type of sample is brought to the laboratory and observed as they continue to grow, as some insects cannot be positively identified until they are fully developed. When insect-related evidence is collected, the forensic entomologist does more than just find and transfer the evidence to the laboratory. They note the location from which the eggs, larvae, and insects are being removed from, the temperature of the eggs/larvae/insects, the temperature of the body on which they were found (if applicable), and environmental factors, such as temperature, humidity, and season of the year. In order to do this, forensic entomologists often sketch diagrams, photograph, or record the scene and collection process, as well as take notes.

Once back in the laboratory, forensic entomologists use tools and instruments, such as a microscope, to examine the eggs/larvae/ insects. They also consult a vast array of entomological research that documents the characteristics of the types of insects being investigated—for example, what geographic locations they are typically found in, the various stages of their life cycles, and how they behave. By using this information and taking into consideration where the body or source of infestation was found, what time of year it is, and the weather, as well as the types of insects/larvae/eggs found and their known life cycles under those conditions, a forensic entomologist can often determine when a victim died, or, in civil cases, when and where an infestation likely began. A forensic entomologist may be asked to testify in legal proceedings about his or her research and conclusions.

REQUIREMENTS
High School
In high school, take courses in biology, ecology, physics, statistics, general science, chemistry, Latin, geometry, and algebra. You should also take English and speech courses to hone your communication skills, which you will use often when writing reports, interacting with coworkers, and testifying in court.

Postsecondary Training
Most forensic entomologists have a doctorate in entomology, zoology, biology, or a related field, although some people are able to find positions with bachelor's or master's degrees. To earn a doctorate,

you must first earn a bachelor's degree in entomology, biology, zoology, ecology, forensic science, or a related field, then go on to earn a master's degree in entomology or a related area. The Entomological Society of America provides a list of colleges and universities that offer courses and degrees at its Web site, http://www.entsoc.org/resources/education.

Once they earn their doctorates, forensic entomologists typically participate in a fellowship that focuses on entomology or forensic entomology. They also continue learning throughout their careers by participating in workshops, seminars, and educational conferences.

Certification or Licensing

The American Board of Forensic Entomology offers voluntary certification to forensic entomologists. There are two status categories: member status and diplomate status. To attain member status, applicants must have earned a master of science degree in entomology, biology, zoology, or ecology; have at least three years of professional experience in the field; have published at least one peer-reviewed publication; and given at least one professional presentation about a topic in forensic entomology. To attain diplomate status, applicants must have met all the requirements for member status; earned a doctoral degree in entomology, biology, zoology, or ecology; have at least five years of professional experience in the field; have published at least three peer-reviewed publications; given at least five professional presentations about a topic in forensic entomology; and pass an examination. Contact the board for more information.

Additionally, the Entomological Society of America offers two certification designations for entomologists who are employed in all fields: associate certified entomologist and board certified entomologist. Contact the society for more information.

Other Requirements

To be a successful forensic entomologist, you should be organized, able to solve problems, enjoy conducting research and analysis, and have an inquisitive personality. You should also have good communication skills in order to write research reports and provide effective testimony in court.

EXPLORING

There are many ways to explore the field of entomology. The American Entomological Society hosts an Annual Insect Field Day, where people of all ages from the Philadelphia, Pennsylvania, area (as well as tourists) can learn about insects by participating in field trips, viewing insect displays and collections, and listening to talks on preparing an insect collection. Visit http://www.ansp.org/hosted/aes/fieldday.htm for more information. Many books and magazines provide information about insects and the field of entomology. There are also many Web sites that feature photographs of insects as well as information about entomology and the specialty of forensic entomology. The Entomological Society of America offers a variety of information about educational programs and publications (such as *Discover Entomology: A Hobby, A Career, a Lifetime)* at its Web site (http://www.entsoc.org). Finally, ask your science teacher or counselor to arrange an information interview with an entomologist or forensic entomologist to help you learn more about these fields.

EMPLOYERS

Forensic entomologists are employed by offices of coroners and medical examiners, law offices, law enforcement agencies, federal government agencies such as the FBI, court systems, and other organizations. Others work for colleges and universities as teachers and researchers. Most forensic entomologists work part time in this specialization, spending the remainder of their time working as educators or as entomologists in other fields. Entomologists who do not specialize in forensic entomology are employed by conservation organizations; colleges and universities; local, state, and federal government agencies (such as the National Park Service and the U.S. Fish and Wildlife Service); and a variety of other employers.

STARTING OUT

You won't start out in your career as a forensic entomologist. It usually takes a couple of years working as a general entomologist to gain experience in entomology and forensic science before you can advertise your expertise as a forensic entomologist.

You can find job leads through your college's career services office, through contacts you have made with professors, and by contacting professional entomological associations. The Entomological Society of America, for example, offers job listings at its Web site (http://www.entsoc.org/employment/jobs.htm).

ADVANCEMENT

Forensic entomologists typically advance by receiving higher pay, more job responsibilities (including managerial duties), or by being asked to work on higher profile cases. Others seek employment at larger law enforcement agencies. Forensic entomologists who are employed in academia advance by working their way through the academic ranks—from instructor to assistant professor to associate professor and finally to full professor. Some professors become department heads or work in other administrative positions.

EARNINGS

There is no comprehensive information available regarding salaries for forensic entomologists, but the U.S. Department of Labor (DoL) does provide information on biologists, not otherwise classified (a category that includes forensic entomologists). The median salary for these professionals was $65,080 in 2008, according to the DoL. Salaries ranged from less than $35,620 to $101,030 or more. In 2008, biological scientists working for the federal government earned a mean annual salary of $70,270, and those employed by state government agencies earned $55,500.

Forensic entomologists who work as consultants are typically paid by the hour, by the day, or receive a flat fee that is determined by the work required.

Benefits for full-time forensic entomologists include vacation and sick time, health, and sometimes dental, insurance, and pension or 401(k) plans. Those who are self-employed must provide their own benefits.

WORK ENVIRONMENT

Forensic entomologists spend much of their time in laboratories and offices analyzing their findings. These places are typically clean and well-ventilated and lighted. Forensic entomologists travel to crime scenes, both indoors and outdoors, to gather evidence. These locations can be stiflingly hot, windy, or wet and rainy. At crime scenes, forensic entomologists often encounter decaying corpses, which may be disturbing. They also travel to courthouses to testify about their findings.

OUTLOOK

Forensic entomology is a small, but growing, field. Employment for forensic entomologists will continue to increase as more law enforcement agencies learn about the benefits of hiring these professionals to help solve cases. Opportunities will be best for those with advanced degrees and certification, as well as a considerable amount of experience in the field.

FOR MORE INFORMATION

For information on forensic careers and education, contact
American Academy of Forensic Sciences
410 North 21st Street
Colorado Springs, CO 80904-2712
Tel: 719-636-1100
http://www.aafs.org

For information on certification, contact
American Board of Forensic Entomology
http://www.forensicentomologist.org

For information on entomology and its field day for people of all ages, contact
American Entomological Society
At the Academy of Natural Sciences
1900 Benjamin Franklin Parkway
Philadelphia, PA 19103-1195
Tel: 215-561-3978
Email: aes@acnatsci.org
http://www.ansp.org/hosted/aes

For information on careers in biology, contact
American Institute of Biological Sciences
1444 I Street, NW, Suite 200
Washington, DC 20005-6535
Tel: 202-628-1500
http://www.aibs.org

For information on education, careers, and certification, contact
The Entomological Society of America
10001 Derekwood Lane, Suite 100
Lanham, MD 20706-4876
Tel: 301-731-4535
Email: esa@entsoc.org
http://www.entsoc.org

Forensic Nurses

QUICK FACTS

School Subjects
Biology
Chemistry
Health

Personal Skills
Helping/teaching
Technical/scientific

Work Environment
Primarily indoors
Primarily multiple locations

Minimum Education Level
Some postsecondary training

Salary Range
$43,410 to $62,450 to
$92,240+

Certification or Licensing
Voluntary (certification)
Required (licensing)

Outlook
Much faster than the average

DOT
075

GOE
10.02.01

NOC
3152

O*NET-SOC
29-1111.00

OVERVIEW

Forensic nursing is a relatively new and expanding field of nursing that combines nursing skills with investigative skills. *Forensic nurses* are trained to work with victims, suspects, and evidence of crimes, and work in a variety of settings. They may have additional titles specific to their occupation. Forensic nurses are registered nurses who have received additional training that prepares them for work in the field. There are approximately 2.5 million registered nurses in the United States. Only a small percentage of registered nurses specialize in forensic nursing.

HISTORY

Modern ideas about hospitals and nursing as a profession did not develop until the 19th century. The life and work of Florence Nightingale were a strong influence on the profession's development. Nightingale, who came from a wealthy, upper-class British family, dedicated her life to improving conditions in hospitals, beginning in an army hospital during the Crimean War. In the United States, many of Nightingale's ideas were put into practice for the care of the wounded during the Civil War. The care, however, was provided by concerned individuals who nursed rather than by trained nurses. They had not received the kind of training that is required for nurses today.

The first school of nursing in the United States was founded in Boston in 1873. In 1938 New York State passed the first state law to require that practical nurses be licensed. After the 1938 law was passed, a movement began to have organized training programs that would assure new standards in the field. The role and training of nurses have undergone radical changes since the first schools were opened.

Nurses have been working with victims of abuse and sexual assault for years, but it was not until 1992 that the term "forensic nurse" was used to describe nurses in this specialty. Seventy-two nurses met at a professional conference hosted by the Sexual Assault Resource Service and the University of Minnesota School of Nursing in Minneapolis, Minnesota, to discuss the field of sexual assault nursing. They quickly realized that they had much in common and that they should form a professional association to represent their interests. The International Association of Forensic Nurses (IAFN) was incorporated in 1993. In 1996 the American Association of Nurses recognized forensic nursing as a specialty of nursing. Today, the IAFN has more than 3,000 members in 24 countries. The association's members work not only in sexual assault examination positions, but in any situations in which people have been abused or an accident has occurred that has caused injury or loss of life.

THE JOB

Forensic nurses use a combination of skills to meet multiple purposes, often serving not only as nurses, but as crime solvers and advocate for victims, too. They are employed in a variety of settings. They may work in hospitals (particularly in emergency rooms) or other health-care facilities, correctional institutions, the offices of medical examiners and coroners, psychiatric facilities, insurance agencies, social service agencies . . . the list goes on. In general, anywhere that a registered nurse might work is a setting in which the skills of a forensic nurse will likely be of use, especially if it is a place where victims or suspects in a crime or accident may be investigated or treated.

In addition to performing general nursing duties, forensic nurses are likely to be involved with additional tasks related to investigations of accidents or crimes. These duties include observing the victims of (and sometimes the scene of) an accident or crime for potential evidence—forensic nurses are generally better trained than other nurses to spot signs of abuse or trauma. They may also examine suspected perpetrators of crimes. A forensic nurse must carefully collect, document, and preserve any evidence they find for any future legal proceedings. Many forensic nurses are called on to provide testimony in court.

There are several specialties in the field of forensic nursing. One of the largest areas of specialization pertains to sexual assault examination. Forensic nurses trained in this area often have an additional title, such as *sexual assault nurse examiner* (SANE), *sexual assault examiner* (SAE), *sexual assault forensic examiner* (SAFE), or *forensic nurse examiner* (FNE). As most of these titles imply, SANEs, SAEs, SAFEs, and FNEs work with survivors of sexual assault. They typically interview the survivors, obtaining their medical history and a thorough account of the assault. The forensic nurse then performs a physical examination, looking for any signs of the assault. Although sometimes signs of trauma are clearly evident, in many cases they are internal and not easily visible without careful examination and special supplies and equipment. Evidence is carefully obtained, documented, and preserved: this may range from collecting fluids, hairs, textiles, or other physical bits of evidence, to recording evidence of trauma, such as taking photographs of bruising or lacerations to the victim's body. Later, the forensic nurse may be called upon to testify in a legal proceeding related to the assault.

Trauma nurses with forensic nursing training typically work in the emergency rooms of hospitals. Their functions are similar to those of SANEs and the related nurses discussed above, but they have a much broader mandate, as they come in contact with many patients and focus on those who may be the victims or perpetrators of domestic violence, other types of abuse, and crimes. *Trauma forensic nurses* examine patients and preserve and or document evidence of the injuries caused by the abuse or crime, or, in the case of a suspected perpetrator, any evidence indicating he or she committed the abuse or crime. They also identify patients who may have attempted suicide or are displaying psychiatric symptoms and help direct them to the mental health care they need.

Forensic nurse investigators are involved in death investigations. They are employed by offices of coroners or medical examiners and work alongside law enforcement personnel at the scene of a death. They may examine the deceased individual and investigate the physical location of and the circumstances surrounding the death. They may also assist in conducting autopsies.

Another area of specialization is legal consulting. Forensic nurses in this area may have an additional title, typically *legal nurse consultant* (LNC). LNCs are much more involved in the legal aspects of investigations than other forensic nurses. They work on a range of cases—usually civil rather than criminal—that deal with such issues as medical malpractice, personal injury, wrongful death, or worker's compensation.

Other forensic nurses work with specific groups of people, such as geriatric, pediatric, incarcerated, or mentally ill populations, focusing on investigating the injuries or deaths caused by the abuse or crimes affecting those groups. In addition, forensic nurses working with mentally ill populations also may be responsible for assessing a person's level of competency (whether it be at the present time, what it might be in the future, or trying to determine what is was at a previous point in time, such as during a criminal incident).

REQUIREMENTS

High School
In order to become a forensic nurse you will first need to become a registered nurse. To prepare for training as a registered nurse, you should take high school mathematics and science courses, including biology, chemistry, and physics. Health courses will also be helpful. English and speech courses should not be neglected because you must be able to communicate well with patients. Psychology classes will be especially useful for aspiring forensic nurses because they often work with people who have been the victims of a crime.

Postsecondary Training
There are three basic kinds of training programs that you may choose from to become a registered nurse: associate's degree, diploma, and bachelor's degree. The choice of which of the three training programs to pursue depends on your career goals. A bachelor's degree in nursing is required for most supervisory or administrative positions, for jobs in public health agencies, and for admission to graduate nursing programs. There are approximately 710 bachelor's degree programs in nursing in the United States. A bachelor's degree in nursing requires four (in some cases, five) years to complete. The graduate of this program receives a bachelor of science in nursing (BSN) degree. The associate degree in nursing (ADN) is awarded after completion of a two-year study program that is usually offered by a junior or community college. There are approximately 850 ADN programs in the United States. You receive hospital training at cooperating hospitals in the general vicinity of the community college. The diploma program, which usually lasts three years, is conducted by hospitals and independent schools, although the number of these programs is declining. At the conclusion of each of these programs, you become a graduate nurse, but not, however, a registered nurse. To obtain the RN designation you must pass a licensing examination required in all states.

Courses in forensic nursing are often offered as electives during undergraduate training. It is a good idea to take as many of these as possible while an undergraduate.

The next step to becoming a forensic nurse is earning a graduate degree in forensic nursing. The International Association of Forensic

Nurses offers a list of colleges and universities that offer degrees in forensic nursing at its Web site, http://www.iafn.org.

According to The Forensic Nurse Web site, forensic nurses must have "successfully completed a formal didactic educational program in forensic nursing . . . which included a minimum of 40 contact hours in the core areas of forensic nursing. These core areas include the history of forensic nursing; the forensic nursing process; violence and victimology; injury identification, interpretation, and documentation; criminalistics and forensic science; and nursing and the interdisciplinary process with law enforcement/and legal process."

Certification or Licensing

Voluntary certification is available for a variety of registered nursing specialties. The International Association of Forensic Nurses offers the following voluntary certifications to forensic nurses: SANE-A (for sexual assault nurse examiners of adults and adolescents) and SANE-P (for sexual assault nurse examiners that care for pediatric and adolescent populations). Applicants must satisfy experience requirements and pass an examination. Certification must be renewed every three years.

The International Association of Forensic Nurses is currently working with the American Nurse Credentialing Center (http://www.nursecredentialing.org) to develop the advanced practice forensic nurse portfolio credential.

The American College of Forensic Examiners offers the voluntary certified forensic nurse designation to those who satisfy experience and education requirements and pass an examination.

Certification as a legal nurse consultant certified is voluntary and is available through the American Legal Nurse Consultant Certification Board. This credential demonstrates that the legal nurse consultant has met practice experience requirements and has passed an examination testing all areas of legal nurse consulting. The certificate is renewed every five years through continuing education or reexamination and continued practice in the specialty.

All states and the District of Columbia require a license to practice nursing. To obtain a license, graduates of approved nursing schools must pass a national examination. Nurses may be licensed by more than one state. In some states, continuing education is a condition for license renewal. Different titles require different education and training levels.

Other Requirements

You should have a strong desire to help others, especially those who may experience fear or anger as a result of being abused or a victim of a crime. Patience, compassion, objectivity, and calmness are qualities needed by anyone working in this career. In addition, you must have excellent observational and communication skills, be detail oriented, and be able to give directions as well as follow instructions and work as part of a health care team. Anyone interested in becoming a forensic nurse should also have a strong desire to continue learning because new tests, procedures, and technologies are constantly being developed.

EXPLORING

You can explore your general interest in nursing in a number of ways. Read books on careers in nursing and talk with high school counselors, school nurses, and local public health nurses. Visit hospitals to observe the work and talk with hospital personnel to learn more about the daily activities of nursing staff.

Some hospitals now have extensive volunteer service programs in which high school students may work after school, on weekends, or during vacations in order to both render a valuable service and to explore their interests. There are other volunteer work experiences available with the Red Cross or community health services. Camp counseling jobs sometimes offer related experiences. Some schools offer participation in Future Nurses programs.

The Internet is full of resources about nursing. Check out Discover Nursing (http://www.discovernursing.com), Nursing Net (http://www.nursingnet.org), and the American Nursing Association's Nursing World (http://www.nursingworld.org).

You won't be able to explore work as a forensic nurse directly, but there are still many ways to learn about the field. In addition to the general suggestions made earlier about exploring nursing, you can also read books about forensic nursing, such as *Forensic Nurse: The New Role of the Nurse in Law Enforcement,* by Serita Stevens and visit Web sites about forensic nursing, such as The Forensic Nurse (http://www.theforensicnurse.com). You should also ask your health teacher or school counselor to help arrange an information interview with a forensic nurse.

EMPLOYERS

Approximately 2.5 million registered nurses are employed in the United States, but only a very small percentage of RNs work as forensic nurses. Employers of forensic nurses include hospitals (particularly in emergency rooms) and other health-care facilities, offices of medical examiners and coroners, correctional institutions, law firms, psychiatric facilities, insurance agencies, and social service agencies. Twenty-one percent of all nurses work part time.

STARTING OUT

The only way to become a registered nurse is through completion of one of the three kinds of educational programs, plus passing the licensing examination. Registered nurses may apply for employment directly to hospitals, nursing homes, home care agencies, temporary nursing agencies, companies, and government agencies that hire nurses. Jobs can also be obtained through school career services offices, by signing up with employment agencies specializing in placement of nursing personnel, or through state employment offices. Other sources of jobs include nurses' associations, professional journals, and newspaper want ads.

The International Association of Forensic Nurses provides job listings at its Web site (http://iafn.associationcareernetwork.com/Common/HomePage.aspx).

ADVANCEMENT

Increasingly, administrative and supervisory positions in the nursing field go to forensic nurses who have earned at least a bachelor of science in nursing. Forensic nurses with many years of experience who are graduates of a diploma program may achieve supervisory positions, but requirements for such promotions have become more difficult in recent years and in many cases require at least the BSN degree.

EARNINGS

Forensic nurses may earn a regular salary, be paid per case, or be paid by the hour. The U.S. Department of Labor does not provide salary information for forensic nurses, but it does provide information on earnings for registered nurses. In 2008 registered nurses had median annual earnings of $62,450. Salaries ranged from less than $43,410 to more than $92,240. Those who worked at hospitals had mean annual earnings of $66,490, and those employed at nursing care facilities earned $58,360. According to The Forensic Nurse Web site, forensic nurses may be paid anywhere from $150 to $400 per case. Other forensic nurses may receive hourly salaries that range from $25 per hour to $100 per hour or more.

Salaries for forensic nurses are determined by several factors: setting, education, and work experience. Most full-time forensic nurses are given flexible work schedules as well as health and life insurance; some are offered education reimbursement and year-end bonuses. Many forensic nurses take advantage of overtime work and shift differentials. About 7 percent of all nurses hold more than one job.

WORK ENVIRONMENT

Most forensic nurses work in facilities that are clean and well lighted and where the temperature is controlled, although some work in rundown inner city hospitals in less-than-ideal conditions.

Forensic nurses spend much of their work day on their feet, either walking or standing. Assisting patients who have been sexually assaulted or otherwise abused, as well as working with criminal offenders, can be very stressful and exhausting. Despite this, forensic nurses must maintain their composure and focus on doing their jobs and helping crime victims receive justice.

Forensic nurses who work in hospital emergency rooms and clinics that handle sexual assault cases may be on call, which often involves being called to work on evenings and weekends. They may have to travel to the scene of a crime and to court to testify regarding their findings.

OUTLOOK

The nursing field is the largest of all health care occupations, and employment prospects for nurses are excellent. The U.S. Department of Labor projects that employment for registered nurses will grow much faster than the average for all professions through 2016.

Opportunities should also be very strong for forensic nurses. This profession is growing quickly as a result of increases in crime. There is currently a shortage of experienced forensic nurses, which is creating demand for qualified professionals. Registered nurses with graduate degrees and/or certificates in forensic nursing will have the best employment prospects.

FOR MORE INFORMATION

For information about forensic nursing, contact
Academy of Forensic Nursing Science
Tel: 760-322-9925
Email: info@tafns.com
http://www.academyofforensicnursingscience.com

Visit the AACN Web site to access a list of member schools and to read the online pamphlet Your Nursing Career: A Look at the Facts.

American Association of Colleges of Nursing (AACN)
One Dupont Circle, Suite 530
Washington, DC 20036-1135
Tel: 202-463-6930
http://www.aacn.nche.edu

For information on certification and to read Getting Started in Legal Nurse Consulting: An Introduction to the Specialty, *visit the AALNC Web site.*

American Association of Legal Nurse Consultants (AALNC)
401 North Michigan Avenue
Chicago, IL 60611-4255
Tel: 877-402-2562
Email: info@aalnc.org
http://www.aalnc.org

For information on forensic science and certification, contact
American College of Forensic Examiners
2750 East Sunshine Street
Springfield, MO 65804-2047
Tel: 800-423-9737
http://www.acfei.com

For information about opportunities as an RN, contact the following organizations:
American Nurses Association
8515 Georgia Avenue, Suite 400
Silver Spring, MD 20910-3492
Tel: 800-274-4262
http://www.nursingworld.org

American Society of Registered Nurses
1001 Bridgeway, Suite 411
Sausalito, CA 94965-2104
Tel: 415-331-2700
Email: office@asrn.org
http://www.asrn.org

Discover Nursing, sponsored by Johnson & Johnson Services Inc., provides information on nursing careers (including forensic nursing), nursing schools, and scholarships.
Discover Nursing
http://www.discovernursing.com

Visit the association's Web site for information on educational programs, careers, and certification.
International Association of Forensic Nurses
1517 Ritchie Highway, Suite 208
Arnold, MD 21012-2323
Tel: 410-626-7805
http://www.iafn.org

For information about state-approved programs and information on nursing, contact the following organizations:
National League for Nursing
61 Broadway, 33rd Floor
New York, NY 10006-2701
Tel: 800-669-1656
http://www.nln.org

National Organization for Associate Degree Nursing
7794 Grow Drive
Pensacola, FL 32514-7072
Tel: 850-484-6948
http://www.noadn.org

Forensic Odontologists

QUICK FACTS

School Subjects
Biology
Chemistry
Health
Mathematics
Physics

Personal Skills
Technical/scientific

Work Environment
Primarily indoors
Primarily one location

Minimum Education Level
Medical degree

Salary Range
$46,600 to $137,970 to
$300,200+

Certification or Licensing
Recommended (certification)
Required by all states
(licensing)

Outlook
About as fast as the average

DOT
072

GOE
14.03.01

NOC
3113

O*NET-SOC
29-1021.00, 29-1029.00

OVERVIEW

Dentists maintain their clients' teeth through such preventive and restorative practices as extracting, filling, cleaning, or replacing teeth. They perform corrective work, such as straightening teeth, and treat diseased tissue of the gums. They also perform surgical operations on the jaw or mouth, and make and fit false teeth, as well as cosmetic procedures such as crowns, bleaching, and porcelain veneers. *Forensic odontologists* are specialized dentists who help identify human remains and compare bite marks to a particular individual. Only a small percentage of dentists specialize in forensic odontology.

HISTORY

Teeth are some of the strongest parts of our bodies, which make them resistant to destruction by fire, decay, or other damaging processes. Because of this durability they have been used to identify the dead for hundreds, if not thousands, of years. Hundreds of years ago, forensic odontology concepts were often used to identify the dead—especially in times of war. For example, the corpse of Charles, Duke of Burgundy was identified in 1477 A.D. in France by the absence of certain teeth (as well as the presence of old battle scars). During the Revolutionary War (1775–1783) Paul Revere, American patriot and dentist, used dental records to identify soldiers killed in battle.

Teeth and bite-marks were also studied to solve crimes. In 1850 in the United States, Dr. John White Webster was the first person to be convicted of murder as a result of the study of dental evidence. Authorities found a jawbone with false teeth and other human remains at a laboratory where the doctor worked. The body parts were matched to the man who was murdered, and Dr. Webster was found guilty and executed by hanging. Nearly one hundred years later in 1948, the English pathologist Cedric Keith Simpson solved a murder case using bite-mark evidence. This is one of the first recorded examples of bite-marks being used to convict a defendant in court.

Forensic odontologists have also played a major role in accident and mass murder investigations such as the crash of American Airlines Flight 191 near Chicago, Illinois, in 1979; the cult mass suicide/murders led by Jim Jones at Jonestown, Guyana, in 1979; and the terrorist attacks in the United States in 2001 at multiple locations. The work of forensic odontologists has been critical to the identification of soldiers and civilians killed in wars, including World War II, the Korean War, the Vietnam War, and the Iraq War. They also have played a significant role identifying victims of natural disasters such as the Asian Tsunami (2004) and Hurricane Katrina (2005).

Today, forensic odontologists continue to play a key role in identifying the dead and solving crimes. Their role will only expand as technology innovations improve their ability to analyze evidence.

THE JOB

Forensic odontologists (also referred to as *forensic dentists*) work with medical examiners or police investigators, examining and evaluating dental evidence to identify human remains that often cannot be identified any other way. Forensic dentists are frequently called in for their identification skills after natural disasters such as Hurricane Katrina that result in numerous fatalities. Another important part of the forensic dentist's job is to assess and try to determine the source of bite-mark injuries. Forensic odontologists can also be of service in dental malpractice or dental insurance fraud investigations, and they must be certain enough of their conclusions to testify about them in court if necessary.

Forensic dentists perform identification of human remains by comparing the teeth of a deceased person to dental records or antemortem (prior to death) radiographs (x-rays). A dental computer system called WinID, which links to a Microsoft Access database, helps match missing persons to unidentified human remains. It stores dental and other characteristics—such as restored dental surfaces, physical descriptors, and other pathological findings—for a great number of people and has extensive data-filtering and data-sorting capabilities.

Forensic dentists also evaluate bite marks, which may be left by an attacker on a victim of a crime, by the victim on the perpetrator, or on an object found at a crime scene. Bite marks are sometimes found on children or elderly people who are being abused. The forensic dentist first obtains a saliva sample from the bite if possible for the possibility of gathering DNA. Next, he or she will take photographs, taking care to get the lighting, color, and camera angle right. Next, the forensic dentist makes multiple impressions, casts, or molds of the bite mark, using a variety of rubber-type materials. Computerized bite-analysis software also exists that requires a strong working knowledge of Adobe Photoshop. Once a suspect is apprehended, the forensic dentist makes one or more impressions of the suspect's teeth, comparing them to the recorded bite marks in hopes of finding a match.

In addition to marks on human skin, bite marks on foods such as apples and cheese, on duct tape, on pencils, or even on a steering wheel can yield valuable information. Forensic dentists may analyze animal bites as well, including those of dogs, mountain lions, and sharks.

REQUIREMENTS
High School
If you are considering a career as a forensic dentist, be sure to study biology, chemistry, physics, health, mathematics, and forensic science (if available) in high school. English and foreign language courses are also important for meeting college entrance requirements and developing good communications skills. Participation in extracurricular activities will also enhance your background because they provide opportunities to interact with many different people and develop interpersonal skills.

Postsecondary Training
The first step to becoming a forensic odontologist is to attend dental school. The dental profession is selective, and standards are high. Your college grades and the amount of college education you have completed at the time of application are carefully considered in the admissions process for dental school. In addition, all dental schools approved by the American Dental Association require applicants to pass the Dental Admissions Test, which gauges a student's prospects of success or failure in dental school. Information on tests and testing centers may be obtained from the Council on Dental Education and Licensure of the American Dental Association.

Dental schools require at least two years of college-level predental education. However, about 80 percent of students entering dental schools have already earned a bachelor's or master's degree. Professional training in a dental school generally requires four academic years. Many dental schools have an interdisciplinary curriculum in which the dental student studies basic science with students of medicine, pharmacy, and other health professions. Clinical training is frequently begun in the second year. Generally the degree of doctor of dental surgery (DDS) is granted upon graduation, although some schools give the degree of doctor of dental medicine (DMD).

Once you earn your DDS or DDM, you will prepare for the field of forensic dentistry by enrolling in postgraduate study that lasts from two to five years. A small number of dental schools offer courses in forensic odontology, which cover topics such as evidence collection and handling, autopsy protocol, disaster victim identification, and legal report writing. The American Academy of Forensic Sciences offers a list of colleges and professional associations that offer coursework and workshops in forensic odontology at its Web site (http://www.aafs.org). The American Dental Association provides a list of general dental education programs at its Web site (http://www. ada.org).

Certification or Licensing

The American Board of Forensic Odontology provides voluntary certification to forensic odontologists who have a DDS, DMD, or equivalent dental degree from an accredited academic institution; satisfy experience requirements; and pass a written practical and oral examination. The American College of Forensic Examiners offers certification in a variety of categories, including certified medical investigator and certified forensic consultant. Contact these organizations for more information.

All 50 states and the District of Columbia require dentists to be licensed. To qualify for a license in most states, a candidate must graduate from a dental school accredited by the American Dental Association's Commission on Dental Accreditation and pass written and practical examinations. Candidates may fulfill the written part of the exam by passing the National Board Dental Examinations. Individual states or regional testing agencies give the written or practical examinations. Generally, dentists licensed in one state are required to take another exam to practice in another state. However, 20 states grant licenses to dentists from other states based on their credentials. Dentists who intend to practice in a specialty area must be licensed or certified in certain states.

Other Requirements

Manual dexterity and scientific ability are important skills for forensic odontologists. They also need strong writing skills in order to communicate their findings effectively, as well as excellent verbal communication skills in order to testify in court. Good vision is required because of the detailed work.

EXPLORING

You might be able to gain an awareness of the demands of dentistry by observing a dentist at work. Work as a dental hygienist, dental assistant, or dental laboratory technician might lead to continued study in dentistry. Also, consider volunteering in any medical environment to gain a feel for medical work. Even if you volunteer at a local hospital, for example, you'll be able to work around medical staff and discover firsthand how it feels to help people.

To learn more about forensic odontology, read books and magazines about the field. You can also try to volunteer at organizations that specialize in forensic science. Visit Web sites for more information on the field, including ForensicDentistry Online (http://www.forensicdentistryonline.org). You can also visit the Web site of the Bureau of Legal Dentistry (http://www.boldlab.org), "the first and only laboratory in North America that is dedicated to full-time forensic dentistry research, casework and graduate teaching." Another option is to ask your science teacher to arrange an information interview with a forensic dentist.

EMPLOYERS

Forensic odontologists are employed by law enforcement agencies, medical examiners' offices, law firms, insurance companies, government agencies, and dental schools (teaching students or performing research). Forensic dentists who are employed outside of academia typically work part time and are employed on a contract basis. The majority of dentists who do not specialize in forensic odontology work in private practice. Of the remainder, about half work in research or teaching, or hold administrative positions in dental schools. Other opportunities for dentists can be found in the armed forces, public health services, hospitals, and clinics.

STARTING OUT

Most forensic odontologists work as general dentists or as dental educators before they pursue a career in forensic dentistry.

Once a dentist has graduated from an approved dental school and passed a state licensing examination, there are three common avenues of entry into private practice. A dentist may open a new office, purchase an established practice, or join another dentist or group of dentists to gain further experience. There are, however, other choices for licensed dentists. They may enter the armed forces as commissioned officers, or, through civil service procedures, become eligible for work in the U.S. Public Health Service. They may also choose to work in hospitals, clinics, or in dental laboratories.

ADVANCEMENT

Forensic odontologists typically advance by receiving higher salaries or consulting fees for their work and by being asked to work on high-profile cases. Educators may look forward to promotions to administrative positions or to appointments as professors.

EARNINGS

The U.S. Department of Labor does not provide salary data for forensic odontologists, but it does provide information on earnings for dental specialists, not otherwise classified. Ten percent of specialists earned less than $46,600 in 2008. Specialists had median earnings of $137,970. According to the American Dental Association, dental specialists average approximately $300,200 per year.

Forensic odontologists who work as consultants often are paid by the hour. Hourly salaries range from $125 per hour to $500 per hour.

Forensic odontologists who are employed full time by law enforcement agencies, medical examiners' offices, and other organizations receive fringe benefits such as health and life insurance and a savings and pension program. Self-employed forensic dentists must provide their own benefits.

WORK ENVIRONMENT

The offices and laboratories of forensic dentists are usually clean, modern, and feature the latest scientific technology. They sometimes work outside these settings at crime scenes—both outdoors and indoors. Forensic odontologists may have to hike to the scene of a crime and bend or stretch to examine the remains of crime victims. They may be exposed to hazardous materials or communicable diseases; for this reason, they often wear protective equipment such as respirators. Forensic dentists may be assisted by forensic dental assistants, laboratory workers, and other dental personnel.

OUTLOOK

Employment of general dentists is expected to grow about as fast as the average for all occupations through 2016, according to the U.S. Department of Labor. Many positions will open as a result of the need to replace the large number of dentists who reach retirement age or who choose to stay in practice while reducing their office hours. Employment for forensic odontologists is also expected to be good. Although this is a small profession, there is steady demand for dentists with specialized training in forensic dentistry. Those who are willing to travel to take positions or consulting jobs will have the best employment prospects.

FOR MORE INFORMATION

For information on forensic careers, education, and its membership section for odontologists, contact
American Academy of Forensic Sciences
410 North 21st Street
Colorado Springs, CO 80904-2712
Tel: 719-636-1100
http://www.aafs.org

For information on certification, contact
American Board of Forensic Odontology
410 North 21st Street
Colorado Springs, CO 80904-2798
Tel: 719-636-1100
Email: contact@abfo.org
http://www.abfo.org

For information on forensic science and certification, contact
American College of Forensic Examiners
2750 East Sunshine Street
Springfield, MO 65804-2047
Tel: 800-423-9737
http://www.acfei.com

The ADA has information on dental careers (including those in forensic odontology), education requirements, and dental student membership.
American Dental Association (ADA)
211 East Chicago Avenue
Chicago, IL 60611-2678
Tel: 312-440-2500

Email: publicinfo@ada.org
http://www.ada.org

For information on admission requirements of U.S. and Canadian dental schools, contact
American Dental Education Association
1400 K Street, NW, Suite 1100
Washington, DC 20005-2415
Tel: 202-289-7201
Email: adea@adea.org
http://www.adea.org

For information on forensic dentistry, contact
American Society of Forensic Odontology
13048 North Research Boulevard, Suite B
Austin, TX 78750-3205
http://www.asfo.org

INTERVIEW

Adam Freeman, DDS, DABFO is a forensic odontologist and the president of the American Society of Forensic Odontology. He discussed his career and the field with the editors of Careers in Focus: Forensics.

Q. What made you want to enter this career?
A. In the aftermath of the tragedies of 2001, I lost three patients. The town I work in is only a 45-minute commute to New York City. Like everyone in this country I searched for some way to volunteer to make a difference. I found that there was a need for well-trained forensic dentists throughout the country. In 2002 I took the Armed Forces Institute of Pathology's course on forensic pathology and I was hooked. I applied for and was accepted to what is widely known as the most prestigious course of study in the field, a 14-month fellowship at the University of Texas—San Antonio Center for Education and Research in Forensics. The director, Dr. David Senn, who is also the current president of the American Board of Forensic Odontology, was an amazing mentor and now friend.

Q. What are your main and secondary job duties as a forensic odontologist? What type of cases do you work on?
A. Forensic dentists work in several areas, the identification of unknown individuals, the identification of the victims of mass

disasters, bite mark identification, age estimation, as well as expert witnesses in standard of care cases.

Identifications: Forensic dentists, by comparing antemortem (before death) and postmortem (after death) records, aid the medical examiner or coroner in establishing the identity of an individual(s). We use dental radiographs to compare the pattern, shape, and restorative material of dental restorations as well as trabeculation patterns of bone, root formation, and shape pathology, pulp chamber shape and size, and many other features looking for consistencies and inconstancies to narrow down the population of potential victims.

Mass Disasters: In mass disasters we handle identifications on a larger scale. We have a national disaster team in the United States, which is part of the National Disaster Medical Service called DMORT, which stands for Disaster Mortuary Operational Response Teams. DMORT consists of forensic experts from many disciplines along with support staff to aid the local authority in cases of mass disasters both natural and manmade. The team sometimes consists of hundreds of individuals coming together to give closure to the families of the victims. For me it is the teamwork of this team that I find so enjoyable. It is truly an "all for one and one for all" attitude.

Bite marks: Often in the commission of a crime (child abuse, assaults, and homicides) either the suspect bites the victim or the victim bites the suspect. We as forensic dentists compare the patterned injury or bite mark to a suspect's teeth and then either profile the biter or report on the probability that a specific person caused the injury.

Age Estimation: Forensic dentists use third molar development, root of development, as well as biochemical markers, to estimate an age range of an individual. This is often used in cases of immigration.

Standard of Care: More often known as malpractice cases. Forensically trained dentists will often be hired by either the plaintiff or defendant to review cases of suspected malpractice and report on his or her findings.

Q. What are some of the pros and cons of work as a forensic odontologist?

A. Very few dentists practice forensic odontology as a full-time career; most are practicing some form of clinical or academic dentistry and do this as an avocation. It is something that allows a dentist to apply his or her skill and knowledge of dentistry to the law. I cannot think of any con to the field.

Q. What advice would you give to high school students who are interested in this career?

A. Admission into dental school is very competitive, therefore I would recommend doing well in college. Major in something that you enjoy and take the requisite courses necessary for admission into dental school. Study hard for the Dental Aptitude Test because it is an easy way for dental schools to compare candidates. Once in dental school seek out a forensic mentor in your area. If you join the American Society of Forensic Odontology (http://www.asfo.org), which as a student only costs $15, you can do a member search in your area for individuals who work in the field. Contact them and let them know of your interest; mentorship is a large part of the learning process in forensic odontology and many of us are honored to mentor interested parties.

Q. Can you tell us about the American Society of Forensic Odontology? How important is membership to career success?

A. The American Society of Forensic Odontology (ASFO) is one of the oldest and largest forensic dental organizations in the world. It was started in 1971, and is open to all who have an interest. Our Web site is our main form of communication; we have a member section where we post a quarterly newsletter and post a case of the quarter, and it is where members can search for others in their area. We also publish a book, the *Manual of Forensic Odontology,* which is the bible of forensic dentistry. Additionally we have an annual meeting in conjunction with the American Academy of Forensic Sciences, where we present an all-day meeting discussing some aspect of forensic dentistry. There is also a board certifying agency, the American Board of Forensic Odontology. Since its inception in 1976 only 145 people have successfully challenged the board. It is an amazing group of individuals, and I am most proud to be one of them.

To have been elected president of the ASFO is one of the biggest honors of my professional career. I have the utmost respect for the members of the organization who so freely give of their time to work in this field, and to be elected the leader of the largest organization of its type was a thrill.

Forensic Pathologists

OVERVIEW

Pathologists are physicians who analyze tissue specimens to identify abnormalities and diagnose diseases. *Forensic pathologists* are specialists who typically examine the deceased (usually those who die unexpectedly, suddenly, or violently) to determine cause and manner of death.

HISTORY

During the late Middle Ages, the earliest known autopsies were performed to determine cause of death in humans. As these autopsies were documented, much information about human anatomy was gathered and studied. In 1761 the culmination of autopsy material resulted in the first textbook of anatomy by Giovanni Batista Morgagni.

Many developments in pathology occurred during the 19th century, including the discovery of the relationship between clinical symptoms and pathological changes. By the mid-1800s Rudolf Virchow had established the fact that cells, of which all things are composed, are produced by other living cells. He became known as the founder of cellular pathology. Louis Pasteur and Robert Koch later developed the bacteriologic theory, which was fundamental to understanding disease processes. By the late 19th century pathology was a recognized medical specialty.

One of the early pioneers of forensic pathology was Thomas Wakley, a British surgeon and medical reformer. According to an article from the U.S. National Library of Medicine, coroners in England were required by law to "make a public 'view of the body' before jurors and witnesses at the crime scene or other accessible place." If well-known individuals were linked to a death, this inquest was often held in secret or not at all. Wakley strongly disagreed with this practice and worked to change it after he was elected coroner in 1839. Later that year, a worker named Thomas Austin fell into a copper vat of boiling water. His employers quickly buried his body. Wakely ordered Austin's body exhumed so that he could perform an autopsy. According to the U.S. National Library of Medicine, "the coroner's jury ruled that Austin's death was accidental, but that the . . . authorities' negligence, in not placing railings around the vat, had been a contributory factor."

By the late 1800s death investigations, which had often been haphazard and unscientific, were replaced by careful studies conducted by trained physicians with knowledge of pathological anatomy and toxicology. The field continued to grow in the 20th century as medical knowledge increased and the legal system became more complex.

Today forensic pathologists—aided by technological advances ranging from electron microscopes to computers—play an important role in death investigations of all types. According to the U.S. National Library of Medicine, pathologists are now even conducting *virtopsies* (virtual autopsies) that use multi-slice computed tomography and magnetic resonance imaging, combined with 3-D imaging technology, to determine causes of death.

THE JOB

Almost everyone is familiar with the role a forensic pathologist plays in investigating deaths that occur as a result of crime. But what many people may not know is that forensic pathologists investigate many other manners of death as well, including suicides; accidental deaths; deaths that occur under strange circumstances; deaths from natural causes that occur unattended by a physician; deaths that occur in police custody; deaths that occur in prison facilities, hospitals, or other public institutions; deaths that might have been caused by medical malpractice; and deaths resulting from communicable diseases or hazardous products that might pose a threat to public health and safety.

When forensic pathologists investigate a death, they need to gather information about the person who died and the time and place of death. They might go to the scene of the death or where the body was found, noting the circumstances and looking for any evidence that might be present. If they do not visit the scene of death, they

A forensic pathologist points to her head to indicate the bullet entry and exit points she observed on the head of a murder victim. *(Jason Towlen, AP Photo)*

review the findings of the investigators who did. They also study the medical history of the deceased, when available, for any clues it might provide in the death investigation.

The body of the deceased is then moved to the location where a forensic (or microlegal) autopsy or postmortem examination will be performed. First, the forensic pathologist performs a thorough visual inspection of the outside of the body, noting the physical description of the deceased and other things, such as any clothing, jewelry, and tattoos, scars, or other distinguishing marks. They then check for outward signs of injuries, noting location, size, and appearance. For example, they might discover bruising around the neck, an abrasion on the arm, or broken fingernails. Then the forensic pathologist conducts an internal examination of the body. They make an incision on the body, remove the internal organs, and examine them for any clues to the cause of death. Tissue samples from the organs and other items from the body—such as blood, urine, or stomach contents—are removed and then sent to a laboratory, where abnormalities might be discovered. X-rays might also be taken.

Throughout the process, the body is photographed, and the forensic pathologist must maintain detailed notes of the procedure and his or her observations. After the physical examination is complete and lab results are available (which may take several days or weeks), the forensic pathologist compiles his or her findings in a detailed report, indicating, if possible, the cause of death. Sometimes a forensic pathologist is required to give testimony in court about the results of an autopsy. If a body is badly decomposed and/or the identity of the person is unknown, a forensic pathologist might work with other professionals, such as a forensic odontologist (dentist) or a forensic anthropologist, to establish the person's identity and the cause of death.

Some forensic pathologists work with the living. *Clinical forensic pathologists* work with law enforcement and other medical officials to determine patterns of injuries in patients, such as those caused by the abuse or neglect of children or seniors, and other vulnerable populations. Others work with victims of sexual assault.

Forensic pathologists may hold different titles, such as *coroner, medicolegal death investigator,* or *medical examiner.* However, not every professional with one of these other titles is necessarily a forensic pathologist. Forensic pathologists are required to have a medical degree (either an MD or DO) and board certification in forensic pathology.

REQUIREMENTS

High School

If you are interested in becoming a pathologist, you will need to earn a medical degree. Your first step in reaching this goal is taking a college preparatory curriculum in high school. Science courses, such as biology, chemistry, and physics, are necessary, as are math courses. These classes will not only provide you with an introduction to basic science and math concepts, but also allow you to determine your own aptitude in these areas. Especially important are any courses emphasizing laboratory work. Since college will be your next educational step, it is also important to take English courses to develop your researching and writing skills. Foreign language and social science classes will also help make you an appealing candidate for college admission as well as prepare you for your future undergraduate and graduate education. Courses in computer science are a must as well.

Postsecondary Training

Like any medical specialist, a forensic pathologist must earn an MD degree and become licensed to practice medicine, after which begins a four- or five-year pathology residency. There are three options available to prepare for a career as a forensic pathologist, according to the National Association of Medical Examiners. Residents may choose to spend three years studying anatomic pathology followed by one year studying forensic pathology. The second option would include a combination of anatomic pathology, clinical pathology, and forensic pathology. This path lasts five years. The third option, which lasts four years, includes a combination of anatomic pathology, forensic pathology, and toxicology, neuropathology, or a related field. The Intersociety Council for Pathology Information offers a directory of pathology educational programs at its Web site (http://www.pathologytraining.org).

Certification or Licensing

All physicians must be licensed to practice medicine. The American Board of Pathology is the governing board for pathologist certification. A pathologist can pursue certification along three primary paths—an anatomic pathology program, a clinical pathology program, or a combined anatomic and clinical pathology program. Once a pathologist has completed the certification process, he or she can choose to specialize in a particular area of pathology, such as forensic pathology. Gaining certification in a specialty area generally requires an additional one to two years of training, although there is a potential for combining this training with the standard pathology residency program.

Other Requirements

Successful forensic pathologists should have an eye for detail and be able to concentrate intently on work, work well and communicate effectively with others, and be able to accept a great deal of responsibility. They need to perform well under pressure, be patient, thorough, and confident in decisions.

EXPLORING

To learn more about this career, ask your biology teacher or counselor to set up an information interview with a forensic pathologist. Read as many books and other publications as you can about pathology and the specialization of forensic pathology. Visit the Web sites of the associations listed at the end of this article for more information.

EMPLOYERS

Most forensic pathologists work for local, state, and federal governments assisting law enforcement agencies. Some are employed by private hospitals or other medical groups that have government contracts to perform forensic autopsies. Others work at colleges and universities. Pathologists who are not employed in the forensic science specialty work at community hospitals, physicians and medical clinics affiliated with the hospitals, postsecondary institutions, federal government agencies (such as the National Institutes of Health and the Food and Drug Administration), and independent laboratories. Others work in private practice.

STARTING OUT

There are no shortcuts to entering the medical profession. Requirements are an MD degree, a licensing examination, a one- or two-year internship, and a four- or five-year residency. Upon completing this program, which may take up to 13 years, pathologists are then ready to enter practice. Many medical students learn about opportunities from their college career services office or teachers. The National Association of Medical Examiners also lists job opportunities at its Web site (http://www.thename.org).

ADVANCEMENT

Forensic pathologists who are employed by local, state, and federal governments advance by receiving regular raises, managerial duties, or by being assigned to work on high-profile cases. A forensic pathologist working in an academic capacity may advance to direct a medical school's pathology program or head its academic department. Some pathologists open independent pathology laboratories or join with other physicians to form private group practices.

Because pathologists have broad medical perspectives, they often serve in leadership positions in medical schools, professional societies, and research organizations.

EARNINGS

Pathologists employed in all fields earned a median annual salary of $234,230 in 2009, according to Salary.com. Salaries ranged from less than $151,572 to $308,182 or more. Several factors influence earnings, including years of experience, geographic region of practice, and reputation.

Benefits include paid vacation, health, disability, life insurance, and retirement or pension plans. Self-employed forensic pathologists must provide their own benefits.

WORK ENVIRONMENT

The offices and laboratories of most pathologists are well equipped, well lighted, and well ventilated. Forensic pathologists usually work a 40-hour week, but they may be called at any time of the day or night when a crime occurs and an autopsy is required. In addition to their medical duties, forensic pathologists who are self employed or who are in a small group practice must focus on business aspects such as paperwork, supervising staff, and marketing their services.

OUTLOOK

According to the *Occupational Outlook Handbook,* employment for physicians is expected to grow faster than the average for all careers through 2016. The outlook for careers in forensic pathology will also be good. Technological developments have made it easier for forensic pathologists to do their work, which should increase the number of cases that are solved. Opportunities may be reduced if funding for government agencies, which employ the majority of forensic anthropologists, is reduced.

FOR MORE INFORMATION

For information on forensic careers, education, and its membership section for forensic pathologists, contact
   American Academy of Forensic Sciences
   410 North 21st Street
   Colorado Springs, CO 80904-2712
   Tel: 719-636-1100
   http://www.aafs.org

For information on certification, contact
   American Board of Pathology
   PO Box 25915
   Tampa, FL 33622-5915
   Tel: 813-286-2444
   Email: questions@abpath.org
   http://www.abpath.org

For information on pathology careers, contact
   American Society for Clinical Pathology
   33 West Monroe Street, Suite 1600
   Chicago, IL 60603-5617

Tel: 312-541-4999
http://www.ascp.org

Visit the ASIP Web site for information on training programs and to read Pathology: A Career in Medicine.
American Society for Investigative Pathology (ASIP)
9650 Rockville Pike
Bethesda, MD 20814-3993
Tel: 301-634-7130
Email: asip@asip.org
http://www.asip.org

For information on pathology, contact
College of American Pathologists
325 Waukegan Road
Northfield, IL 60093-2750
Tel: 800-323-4040
http://www.cap.org

For information on pathology training programs in the United States and Canada, contact
The Intersociety Committee on Pathology Information
9650 Rockville Pike
Bethesda, MD 20814-3993
Tel: 301-634-7200
Email: ICPI@asip.org
http://www.pathologytraining.org

For comprehensive information on the career of forensic pathologist, visit the association's Web site.
National Association of Medical Examiners
430 Pryor Street, SW
Atlanta, GA 30312-2716
Tel: 404-730-4781
http://www.thename.org

For information on membership, contact
United States and Canadian Academy of Pathology
3643 Walton Way Extension
Augusta, GA 30909-4507
Tel: 706-733-7550
Email: iap@uscap.org
http://www.uscap.org

INTERVIEW

Dr. John Howard is the president of the National Association of Medical Examiners. He discussed his career and the field of forensic pathology with the editors of Careers in Focus: Forensics.

Q. What made you want to enter this career?

A. I was inspired to pursue a career in medicine first by having an interest in the sciences that was sparked by one of my grand-fathers, a science teacher, and then by my family physician for whom I have great respect. Once in medical school I greatly enjoyed the study of anatomy, encouraged by the example of an outstanding professor in that field. My interest in pathology developed during a summer medical school elective in anatomic pathology. I was very impressed by the quality of practice and breadth and depth of knowledge of the three pathologists that I worked with. One of the pathologists loaned me a forensic pathology textbook that summer. I read the book cover to cover and my medical interests focused on the specialty. While I had interest in all areas of medicine and surgery, my attention continued to be drawn to forensic pathology.

Q. What are some of the pros and cons about work as a forensic pathologist?

A. Pros: The work of a forensic pathologist serving as a medical examiner is very important, very interesting, and offers the potential for a long, full-time career. Forensic death investigation is a fundamental part of the foundation of a civilized society. The work blends both traditional medical knowledge and knowledge of the forensic sciences in general—a truly fascinating combination.

Cons: The length of training to become a forensic pathologist is more than most people care to endure. The minimum is four years of college followed by four years of medical school followed by at least three years of residency training in anatomic pathology and finally one year of forensic pathology fellowship. Many forensic pathologists have even more years of formal training after medical school (e.g., six years of training after medical school in my case). Most of the jobs are as government employees with salaries that are less than those of most private-practice physicians with similar years of training and specialization. The practice of medicine in general involves long hours and working at night and on weekends and holidays. Forensic pathology is no exception. Also, medical examiners must deal with the increasingly unrealistic expectations of the public to have exact and immediate answers and a general mistrust of government.

Q. What advice would you give to high school students who are interested in this career?

A. Anyone having an interest in this career must first make a commitment to being a physician and to the practice of medicine. Interested individuals should make contact with college premedical advisers to discuss coursework that will meet both medical school entrance requirements and college graduation requirements. The practice of medicine requires well-rounded individuals—not just good science students. Students should seek some practical experience in health care. Medical examiner work involves the preparation of detailed reports and testimony in court. Students should take writing and public speaking courses in college in addition to science and general credit classes. Additional information about medical examiner work is available at the National Association of Medical Examiners' Web site (http://www.thename.org).

Those not wanting to go through such lengthy training may want to consider one of the many other areas of specialization in the forensic sciences. Additional information is available at the American Academy of Forensic Sciences Web site (http://www.aafs.org).

Q. What is the employment outlook for medical examiners?

A. The employment forecast for medical examiners is favorable. Medical examiner work is population based and the population continues to increase, making a need for more medical examiners in the future.

Q. Can you tell us a little about the National Association of Medical Examiners? How important is membership to career success for medical examiners?

A. The National Association of Medical Examiners (NAME) is the national professional organization of physician medical examiners, medical death investigators, and death investigation system administrators who perform the official duties of the medicolegal investigation of deaths of public interest in the United States. NAME was founded in 1966 with the dual purposes of fostering the professional growth of physician death investigators and disseminating the professional and technical information vital to the continuing improvement of the medical investigation of violent, suspicious, and unusual deaths. Growing from a small nucleus of concerned physicians, NAME has expanded its scope to include physician medical examiners and coroners, medical death investigators, and medicolegal system administrators from throughout the United States and other countries.

Membership in NAME facilitates interaction with other medical examiners, providing for the sharing of medical and forensic science information and practical knowledge that helps with career decisions. NAME establishes practice standards and standards for the accreditation of medical examiner offices. Being a member allows an individual to help shape the future of medical examiner work.

Q. What has been one of your most rewarding experiences as a medical examiner?

A. Some years ago I conducted the medical examiner investigation of the death of a woman that led to the discovery of criminal product tampering. The woman had been found unresponsive in her home and received emergency medical care. She was admitted to the hospital and remained in a coma in the intensive care unit until she died two days later. The cause of her condition and death was a mystery. I reviewed the medical information, conducted a forensic autopsy, and worked with the forensic toxicology laboratory. I identified the cause of death as cyanide poisoning. Further investigation led to the identification of over-the-counter-medication capsule tampering as the source of the poison. There was a nationwide recall of the medication. Multiple capsules containing cyanide were found as a result of the recall and lives were saved. The case illustrates how death investigation serves the living.

Forensic Psychiatrists and Psychologists

OVERVIEW

Forensic psychologists and *forensic psychiatrists* are psychologists and psychiatrists with additional training in legal issues who regularly provide the judicial system with their professional psychological and psychiatric expertise in a variety of matters. Only a small number of psychologists and psychiatrists specialize in forensic psychology and psychiatry.

HISTORY

Many consider German-American psychologist Hugo Munsterberg to be the father of forensic psychology. In 1908 he published *On the Witness Stand*, which advocated for the use of psychology in court cases and other legal matters. In his book, Munsterberg said that it was "astonishing that the work of justice is even carried out in the courts without ever consulting the psychologist." While Munsterberg made some good points in *On the Witness Stand*, some of his "scientific" findings were later found to be fabricated or exaggerated, which caused many to not take the field seriously. Additionally, some lawyers and judges did not believe that the testimony and research of psychologists should be used in legal proceedings because they were not medical doctors.

It took nearly two more decades for pioneers in the field to "demonstrate the empirical basis necessary to qual-

QUICK FACTS

School Subjects
Biology
Psychology
Sociology
Speech

Personal Skills
Helping/teaching
Technical/scientific

Work Environment
Primarily indoors
Primarily multiple locations

Minimum Education Level
Master's degree
  (psychologists)
Medical degree (psychiatrists)

Salary Range
$37,900 to $64,140 to
  $106,840+ (psychologists)
$60,120 to $154,200 to
  $189,499+ (psychiatrists)

Certification or Licensing
Voluntary (certification:
  psychologists)
Required for certain positions
  (licensing: psychologists)
Required (certification/
  licensing: psychiatrists)

Outlook
About as fast as the average

DOT
045, 070

GOE
14.02.01

(continues)

ify as evidentiary expert testimony," according to the *Handbook of Psychology: Volume 11: Forensic Psychology,* edited by Alan M. Goldstein. Psychologists began serving as expert witnesses or legal consultants in cases that did not require expert testimony from medical doctors. For example, forensic psychologists contributed to an appendix that was in the legal brief for the landmark case, *Brown v. the Board of Education* (1954). The courts were also becoming more open to allowing psychologists to serve as legal experts in cases where medical doctors traditionally served in this role. In 1962 a U.S. circuit court judge ruled, according to the *Handbook of Psychology: Volume 11: Forensic Psychology,* "that experts on mental disease could not be limited to physicians." This created even more demand for psychologists who could testify in court. In 2001 the American Psychological Association formally approved forensic psychology as a specialty in the field.

One of the most important responsibilities of forensic psychiatrists is to evaluate the mental competence of a person who is involved in a civil matter or criminal proceeding. For hundreds, if not thousands, of years, people have used the "insanity defense" to avoid being punished for crimes, as well as avoid serving in the military or otherwise contributing to society. Of course, there were many individuals who were actually mentally ill, and in many cultures, the mentally ill were not held criminally responsible for their actions. (This, of course, is still true today in most countries.)

Psychiatry emerged as a medical profession in the early 1800s. As the science developed, psychiatrists were asked by law enforcement officials to evaluate the mental competency of individuals who were accused of crimes or involved in other legal matters (such as determining if a person was mentally competent to make medical decisions). One of the first recorded instances of psychiatrists testifying in court occurred during the 1843 trial of Daniel McNaughton, a woodworker who killed Edward Drummond, personal secretary to several British prime ministers. McNaughton had mistakenly shot Drummond believing he was the prime minister. He was caught and put on trial. The psychiatrists interviewed him and determined that he was insane, which they testified to in court. Their testimony contributed to McNaughton being found not guilty by reason of insanity. The investigative methodologies that were implemented to determine that McNaughton was criminally insane are still used today in many countries and U.S. states that use common law. They are called the McNaughton Rules.

For more than 165 years, forensic psychiatrists have provided their expertise in court proceedings and in other settings. Some pioneers in the field of forensic psychiatry include Karl Augustus Menninger, Manfred Guttmacher, William Alanson White, and Bernard Diamond. These men published books on the field, served as expert witnesses in trials that involved the issue of mental competence, and conducted groundbreaking research that advanced their profession. In 1969 the American Academy of Psychiatry and the Law was founded to represent the professional interests of forensic psychiatrists.

Today, forensic psychologists and psychiatrists play an important role in the criminal justice and legal systems, as well as in other settings.

THE JOB

Although psychologists and psychiatrists that specialize in areas other than forensics may be called to participate in legal proceedings from time to time, forensic psychologists and psychiatrists do so regularly. Their work may range across different areas of law, but they most commonly work with criminal and civil matters.

Some psychologists and psychiatrists work outside of the judicial system. Many teach or conduct research. Others have a private practice that includes non-forensic clinical work. Some work with law enforcement officials to assist with creating criminal profiles, meaning that they use their expertise to help create profiles of criminals or crimes, making it easier for law enforcement officials to identify and apprehend suspects.

The following sections detail specific job responsibilities for forensic psychologists and psychiatrists.

Forensic Psychologists

In civil matters, forensic psychologists may offer counseling services to the parties involved in civil proceedings. In criminal matters, forensic psychologists may evaluate defendants and testify regarding their mental state. Forensic psychologists make psychological evaluations based on criminal evidence or behavior and may offer counseling or treatment to parties involved in the proceedings. Because of their expertise, forensic psychologists are also asked to testify in court for other reasons. They may be asked to confirm or dispute the work of other mental health professionals. Forensic psychologists are also employed to explain psychological concepts to juries and judges.

Forensic psychologists also assist lawyers as they prepare cases for trial. They advise them on psychological issues that might impact legal proceedings. They may assess psychological-related testimony or evidence and explain its relevance. They may also assist with jury selection for a trial.

Some forensic psychologists study various aspects of the judicial process—such as interactions among jurors, or how judges typically reach a verdict—to gain an understanding of typical behaviors and thought processes in these situations. They use this information to learn how decisions are made, which in turn can allow the forensic psychologist to make educated guesses as to how a judge or jury might behave in future proceedings and advise their clients accordingly.

Forensic Psychiatrists

In civil matters, forensic psychiatrists may evaluate the mental competence of a person to determine if he or she has the mental ability to make sound legal decisions, such as creating a will, getting married, or refusing medical treatment. They might evaluate a parent or guardian to determine if they should have custody of a child. Forensic psychiatrists also may be involved in assessing if someone needs to be involuntarily hospitalized for psychiatric treatment.

In criminal matters, forensic psychiatrists may conduct psychiatric evaluations of accused criminals and help determine whether or not defendants understand the charges against them and if they can contribute to their own defense. Like forensic psychologists, forensic psychiatrists are often called to testify on whether the accused is mentally fit to stand trial and to provide an assessment of what the mental state of the accused was when the crime occurred. Because of their expertise, forensic psychiatrists are often called to testify in court as expert witnesses for other reasons as well. Sometimes they evaluate the work of other mental health professionals and offer their own opinion, which might be different. Like forensic psychologists, forensic psychiatrists are also employed to explain psychiatric concepts to juries and judges, breaking down complex scientific information into easier understood concepts so juries and judges are better able to grasp the relevance of such information to the case at hand.

Forensic psychiatrists also assist lawyers as they prepare cases for trial. They advise them on psychiatric issues that might affect their case and they evaluate and explain psychiatric-related testimony or evidence. They also assist with jury selection for a trial by observing potential jurors and offering feedback to lawyers about which potential jurors may be more favorable to the lawyer's client.

REQUIREMENTS

High School

If working as a psychologist or psychiatrist sounds interesting to you, you should start preparing yourself for college while you are still in high school. Do this by taking a college preparatory curriculum and concentrating on math and science classes. Biology, chemistry, and physics as well as algebra, geometry, and calculus will all be helpful. You can also start learning about human behavior by taking psychology, sociology, and history classes. In addition, take English classes to develop your communication skills—much of this work involves speaking, listening, and record keeping.

Postsecondary Training

A doctorate in psychology (Ph.D. or Psy.D.) is recommended for aspiring forensic psychologists. Some positions are available to people with a master's degree, but they are jobs of lesser responsibility and lower salaries than those open to people with a doctorate.

Psychology is an obvious choice for your college major, but not all graduate programs require entering students to have a psychology bachelor's degree. Nevertheless, your college studies should include a number of psychology courses, such as experimental psychology, developmental psychology, and abnormal psychology. You should also take classes in statistics as well as such classes as English, foreign language, and history to complete a strong liberal arts education.

Master's degree programs typically take two years to complete. Course work at this level usually involves statistics, ethics, and other topics.

Some doctoral programs accept students with master's degrees; in other cases, students enter a doctoral program with only a bachelor's degree. Because these entrance requirements vary, you will need to research the programs you are interested in to find out their specific requirements. The doctorate degree typically takes between four and seven years to complete for those who begin their studies with only the bachelor's degree. Coursework will include studies in various areas of psychology and research (including work in quantitative research methods). Those who focus on research often complete a year-long postdoctoral fellowship in forensic psychology. Others gain on-the-job training in the specialty. Frequently those who are interested in clinical, counseling, or school psychology will get the Psy.D. because this degree emphasizes clinical rather than research work. In addition, those interested in these three areas should attend a program accredited by the American Psychological Association. Some colleges offer dual education programs that allow you to earn a law degree and a master's degree or doctorate in psychology.

You will need to earn a medical degree if you want to become a psychiatrist. When you are deciding what college to attend, keep in mind that you'll want one with a strong science department, excellent laboratory facilities, and a strong humanities department. You may want to check out the publication *Medical School Admissions Requirements*, by the Association of American Medical Colleges (AAMC), to see what specific college classes you should take in preparation for medical school. Some colleges or universities offer a "pre-med" major; other possible majors include chemistry, biology, forensic science, or criminal justice. No matter what your major, though, you can count on taking biology, chemistry, organic chemistry, physics, and psychology classes. Medical schools look for well-rounded individuals, however, so be sure to take other classes in the humanities and social sciences. The AAMC reports that most people apply to medical school after their junior year of college. Most medical schools require the Medical College Admission Test as part of their application, so you should take this test your junior or even sophomore year.

In medical school, students must complete a four-year program of medical studies and supervised clinical work leading to their MD degrees. Students will once again concentrate on studying the sciences during their first two years; in addition, they will learn about taking a person's medical history and how to do an examination. The next two years are devoted to clinical work, which is when students first begin to see patients under supervision.

After receiving an MD, physicians who plan to specialize in psychiatry must complete a residency. In the first year, they work in several specialties, such as internal medicine and pediatrics. Then they work for three years in a psychiatric hospital or a general hospital's psychiatric ward. Here they learn how to diagnose and treat various mental and emotional disorders or illnesses.

After completing the four-year residency, those who want to become forensic psychiatrists must complete a one- or two-year fellowship in psychiatry and the law. According to the American Psychiatric Association, training includes "work in evaluation competency, the insanity defense, providing court testimony . . . and clinical experiences with patients in jails and prisons." The American Academy of Psychiatry and the Law offers a list of fellowships at its Web site (http://www.aapl.org).

Certification or Licensing

The American Board of Professional Psychology, in cooperation with the American Board of Forensic Psychology, offers voluntary specialty certification in forensic psychology. Requirements for certification include having a doctorate in psychology, meeting professional experience requirements, obtaining professional licensing, participating in appropriate postdoctoral training, and passing an examination. Psychologists in independent practice or those providing any type of patient care, such as clinical, counseling, and school psychologists, must be licensed or certified by the state in which they practice. Because requirements vary, you will need to check with your state's licensing board for specific information.

All physicians must be licensed in order to practice medicine. After completing the MD, graduates must pass the licensing test given by the board of medical examiners for the state in which they want to work. Following their residency, psychiatrists must take and pass a certifying exam in forensic psychiatry given by the American Board of Psychiatry and Neurology.

Other Requirements
To be a successful forensic psychologist or psychiatrist, you must have excellent communication skills in order to testify in court and explain complicated medical concepts to juries, lawyers, and judges. You should also be able to work effectively with patients, some of whom may be mentally ill, violent, or challenging in some other way. Other important traits include good listening skills, emotional stability in order to deal with patients objectively, the ability to listen well, and the ability to work well with others. Those involved in research, for example, should be analytical, detail oriented, and have strong math and writing skills. No matter what their area of focus, however, all psychologists and psychiatrists should be committed to lifelong learning since our understanding of humans is constantly evolving.

EXPLORING

If you are interested in psychology or psychiatry, explore these fields by taking psychology classes in high school and reading all you can about them, including biographies of and works by noted psychologists and psychiatrists. In addition, make an appointment to talk about the profession with a forensic psychologist or psychiatrist. Use the Internet to learn more about mental health issues by visiting Web sites, such as that of Mental Health America (http://www.nmha. org), American Academy of Psychiatry and the Law (http://www. aapl.org), American Psychiatric Association (http://www.psych.org), or the American Psychological Association (http://www.apa.org).

If doing research work sounds appealing to you, consider joining your school's science club, which may offer the opportunity to work on projects, document the process, and work as part of a team.

An excellent way to explore this type of work is to do volunteer work in health care settings, such as hospitals, clinics, or nursing homes. While you may not be taking care of people with psychiatric problems, you will be interacting with patients and health care professionals. As a college student, you may be able to find a summer job as a hospital orderly, nurse's aide, or ward clerk.

EMPLOYERS

Forensic psychologists and psychiatrists work for government agencies (including those in law enforcement), hospitals, prisons, drug rehabilitation centers, law firms, community health centers that offer specialized services, and in private practice. Others teach at colleges and universities.

STARTING OUT

Those psychologists entering the field with only a bachelor's degree will face strong competition for few jobs. The university career services office or a psychology professor may be able to help such a student find a position assisting a psychologist at a health center or other location. Positions beyond the assistant level, however, will be very difficult to attain. Those psychologists graduating from master's or doctorate degree programs will find more employment opportunities. Again, university career services offices may be able to provide these graduates with assistance. In addition, contacts made during an internship may provide job leads. Joining professional organizations and networking with members is also a way to find out about job openings. In addition, these organizations, such as the American Psychology-Law Society, often list job vacancies in their publications for members or at their Web sites.

Psychiatrists in residency can find job leads in professional journals and through professional organizations such as the American Psychiatric Association. Many are offered permanent positions with the same institution where they complete their residency.

ADVANCEMENT

For those forensic psychologists who have bachelor's or master's degrees, the first step to professional advancement is to complete a doctorate degree. After that, advancement will depend on the area of psychology in which the person is working. For example, a forensic psychologist teaching at a college or university may advance through the academic ranks from instructor to professor. Some college teachers who enjoy administrative work become department heads. Forensic psychologists who work for state or federal government agencies may, after considerable experience, be promoted to head a section or department. After several years of experience, many forensic psychologists enter private practice and set up their own consulting firms.

Most forensic psychiatrists advance in their careers by enlarging their knowledge and skills, clientele, and earnings. Those who work in hospitals, clinics, and mental health centers may become administrators. Those who teach or concentrate on research may become department heads.

EARNINGS

Because these fields offer so many different types of employment possibilities, salaries for psychologists and psychiatrists vary greatly. In addition, the typical conditions affecting salaries, such as the person's level of education, professional experience, and location, also apply.

There is no comprehensive salary information available for forensic psychologists and psychiatrists, but several sources offer information on salaries for general psychologists and psychiatrists.

The U.S. Department of Labor reports that clinical, counseling, and school psychologists earned median salaries of $64,140 in 2008. Salaries ranged from less than $37,900 to $106,840 or more. According to Physicians Search, a physician recruitment agency, average starting salaries for psychiatrists ranged from $110,000 to $180,000 in 2009. Psychiatrists who have practiced for three or more years earned salaries that ranged from $121,000 to $189,499. The median salary for psychiatrists was $154,200 in 2008, according to the U.S. Department of Labor. Some psychiatrists earned less than $60,120.

Forensic psychologists and psychiatrists who work as consultants are often paid by the hour or day, or receive a flat rate based on the services that they provide.

Benefits for full-time workers include vacation and sick time, health, and sometimes dental, insurance, and pension or 401(k) plans. Self-employed psychologists and psychiatrists must provide their own benefits.

WORK ENVIRONMENT

Psychologists and psychiatrists work under many different conditions. Those who work as college or university teachers usually have offices in a building on campus. They may teach 12 to 16 hours a week, and spend a considerable amount of time preparing for class, grading exams, and conducting research. Those in private practice typically work in comfortable office settings. Salaried psychologists and psychiatrists work in private hospitals, state hospitals, community mental health centers, and in other settings. Psychologists and psychiatrists who work in public facilities often have heavy workloads.

Psychologists and psychiatrists often travel to courtrooms, prisons, and other settings to do their work. They sometimes work with the mentally ill who may be violent at times. They must be able to keep their composure if verbally or physically assaulted in order to effectively do their jobs. In courtrooms, they have to defend their findings against criticism from opposing attorneys. Some forensic psychologists and psychiatrists may travel to other cities or states to do their work.

OUTLOOK

The U.S. Department of Labor projects that employment for clinical, counseling, and school psychologists will grow faster than the average for all occupations through 2016, with the largest increase in schools, hospitals, social service agencies, mental health centers, substance abuse treatment clinics, consulting firms, and private companies. Many of these areas depend on government funding, however, and could be adversely affected in an economic downswing when spending is likely to be curtailed. Competition for jobs will be tougher for those with master's or bachelor's degrees. Most job candidates with bachelor's degrees, in fact, will not be able to find employment in the psychology field beyond assistant-level jobs at such places as rehabilitation centers. Opportunities for forensic psychologists should also be good, although competition for employment in this small field will be very strong.

The U.S. Department of Labor predicts that employment for all physicians will grow faster than the average for all careers through 2016. Opportunities for psychiatrists in private practice and salaried positions are good. Psychiatrists are also needed as researchers to explore the causes of mental illness and develop new ways to treat it. Employment for forensic psychiatrists should also be good but, like forensic psychologists, the number of workers in this specialty is small and competition will be high for the best positions.

Forensic psychologists and forensic psychiatrists will be increasingly needed in coming years to serve as expert witnesses and to offer legal consulting services to law firms.

FOR MORE INFORMATION

For information on forensic careers, education, and its membership section for psychiatry and behavioral sciences, contact
American Academy of Forensic Sciences
410 North 21st Street
Colorado Springs, CO 80904-2712
Tel: 719-636-1100
http://www.aafs.org

For information on forensic psychiatry, contact
American Academy of Psychiatry and the Law
One Regency Drive
PO Box 30
Bloomfield, CT 06002-0030
Tel: 860-242-5450
http://www.aapl.org

For information on certification, contact
American Board of Forensic Psychology
http://www.abfp.com

For information on certification in forensic psychology, contact
American Board of Professional Psychology
600 Market Street, Suite 300
Chapel Hill, NC 27516-4057
Tel: 919-537-8031
Email: office@abpp.org
http://www.abpp.org

For information on board certification in forensic psychiatry, contact
American Board of Psychiatry and Neurology
2150 East Lake Cook Road, Suite 900
Buffalo Grove, IL 60089-1875
Tel: 847-229-6500
Email: questions@abpn.com
http://www.abpn.com

For information about the American Journal of Forensic Psychology, *contact*
American College of Forensic Psychology
PO Box 130458
Carlsbad, CA 92013-0458

Tel: 760-929-9777
Email: psychlaw@sover.net
http://www.forensicpsychology.org

For more information on becoming a physician, visit the AMA Web site.
American Medical Association (AMA)
515 North State Street
Chicago, IL 60610-4854
Tel: 800-621-8335
http://www.ama-assn.org

For comprehensive information on careers in psychiatry (including forensic psychiatry), contact
American Psychiatric Association
1000 Wilson Boulevard, Suite 1825
Arlington, VA 22209-3901
Tel: 703-907-7300
Email: apa@psych.org
http://www.psych.org

For more information on careers in forensic psychology, contact
American Psychology-Law Society
c/o American Psychological Association
Division 41
PO Box 11488
Southport, NC 28461-3936
Tel: 910-933-4018
http://www.ap-ls.org

To learn more about careers in medicine and how to apply to medical schools, visit the following Web site:
Association of American Medical Colleges
2450 N Street, NW
Washington, DC 20037-1126
Tel: 202-828-0400
http://www.aamc.org

For licensing information, visit the following Web site:
Association of State and Provincial Psychology Boards
PO Box 241245
Montgomery, AL 36124-1245
Tel: 334-832-4580

Email: asppb@asppb.org
http://www.asppb.org

For information on mental health, and to read the newsletter The
Bell, *which contains current information about the field, visit the
organization's Web site.*
Mental Health America
2001 North Beauregard Street, 6th Floor
Alexandria, VA 22311-1748
Tel: 703-684-7722
http://www.nmha.org

For information on mental health issues, contact
National Institute of Mental Health
6001 Executive Boulevard
Bethesda, MD 20892-0001
Tel: 866-615-6464
Email: nimhinfo@nih.gov
http://www.nimh.nih.gov

Forensic Science Educators

QUICK FACTS

School Subjects
Biology
Chemistry
English
Speech

Personal Skills
Communication/ideas
Helping/teaching
Technical/scientific

Work Environment
Primarily indoors
One location with some
travel

Minimum Education Level
Bachelor's degree (secondary
school teachers)
Master's degree (college
professors)

Salary Range
$34,280 to $51,180 to
$80,970+ (secondary
school teachers)
$33,950 to $61,360 to
$123,430+ (college
professors)

Certification or Licensing
Required by all states
(secondary school teachers)
None available (college
professors)

Outlook
About as fast as the average
(secondary school teachers)
Much faster than the average
(college professors)

(continues)

OVERVIEW

Teachers instruct students of all ages. They develop teaching outlines and lesson plans, give lectures, facilitate discussions and activities, keep class attendance records, assign homework, and evaluate student progress. *Forensic science educators* teach high school and college students about forensic science.

HISTORY

As great advances were made in the field of forensic science in the late 1800s, it soon became clear that formalized educational programs were needed to train people for the field. R. A. Reiss, a professor at the University of Lausanne in Switzerland, established one of the first academic programs in forensic science, according to the Forensic Science Timeline, a Web site by Norah Rudin and Keith Inman. The program, which focused on forensic photography, eventually became the Lausanne Institute of Police Science.

In the United States, the first criminology major was established at the University of California at Berkeley in 1937. In 1945 the first technical major in criminalistics was created at the university. Five years later, a school of criminology was founded at the school.

In the past 25 years, scientific and technological advances have helped forensic scientists solve more cases. This has caused a sharp increase in the number of forensic science education programs in the United States as law enforcement agencies increase their forensic science staffs. Today, nearly every college offers at least a course or two in forensic science, with many colleges and universities offering certificates and undergraduate and graduate degrees in forensic science and specialties such as forensic accounting, forensic nursing, and fingerprint classification.

QUICK FACTS

(continued)

DOT
090, 091

GOE
12.03.02, 12.03.03

NOC
4121, 4141

O*NET-SOC
25-1031.00, 25-1199.00

THE JOB

Secondary Level

Very few high school educators focus solely on teaching forensic science to students. In addition to teaching forensic science, secondary school teachers may teach science, English, math, information technology, business, and other courses.

In the classroom, secondary school teachers rely on a variety of teaching methods. They spend a great deal of time lecturing about forensic science, criminalistics, and related topics, but they also facilitate student discussion and develop projects and activities to interest the students in the subject. They show films and videos, use computers and the Internet, and bring in guest speakers (such as crime scene investigators or fingerprint analysts). They assign essays, presentations, and other projects. Each individual subject calls upon particular approaches, and may involve laboratory experiments and field trips (to crime labs, mock crime scenes, and courtrooms).

Outside of the classroom, secondary school teachers prepare lectures, lesson plans, and exams. They evaluate student work and calculate grades. In the process of planning their class, secondary school teachers read textbooks and workbooks to determine reading assignments; photocopy notes, articles, and other handouts; and develop grading policies. They also continue to study alternative and traditional teaching methods to hone their skills. They prepare students for special events and conferences and submit student work to competitions. Some secondary school teachers also have the opportunity for extracurricular work as athletic coaches or science club advisers.

Postsecondary Level

Forensic science professors perform three main functions: teaching, advising, and researching. Their most important responsibility is to teach students. Their role within the department will determine the level of courses they teach and the number of courses per semester. Most professors work with students at all levels, from college freshmen to graduate students. They may head several classes a semester or only a few a year. Though professors may spend fewer than 10 hours a week in the actual classroom, they spend many hours preparing lesson plans, grading assignments and exams, and preparing grade reports. They also schedule office or computer laboratory hours during the week to be available to students outside of regular classes, and they meet with students individually throughout the semester. In the classroom, professors lecture about forensic science and a variety of other topics depending on the course; demonstrate investigative techniques via hands-on activities such as taking fingerprinting or testing for the presence of blood; administer exams; and assign textbook reading and other research. While most professors teach entry-level forensic science classes such as Introduction to Forensic Science, Forensic Science Investigative Techniques, or Introduction to Evidence Collection, some also teach higher-level classes that center on a particular specialty. In a forensics chemistry class, for example, professors may teach students how to use infrared spectrometry and gas liquid chromatography to locate arson accelerants. In some courses, forensic science educators rely heavily on computer laboratories and hands-on field experiences (such as mock crime scenes) to teach course material.

Another important responsibility is advising students. Not all faculty members serve as advisers, but those who do must set aside large blocks of time to guide students through the program. Forensic science educators who serve as advisers may have any number of students assigned to them, from fewer than 10 to more than 100, depending on the administrative policies of the college. Their responsibility may involve looking over a planned program of studies to make sure the students meet requirements for graduation, or it may involve working intensively with each student on many aspects of college life. They may also discuss the different fields of forensic science (such as criminalistics, forensic odontology, forensic nursing, and questioned document examination) with students and help them identify the best career choices.

The third responsibility of college and university faculty members is research and publication. Faculty members who are heavily involved in research programs sometimes are assigned a smaller teaching load. College forensic science educators publish their research findings in various scholarly journals such as the *International Journal of Forensic Science, The American Journal of Forensic Medicine and Pathology,* and *the Journal of Forensic Science.* They also write books based on their research or on their own knowledge and experience in the field. Most textbooks are written by college and university teachers, or forensic science professionals. Publishing a significant amount of work—and participating in high-profile investigations—has been the traditional standard by which assistant forensic science professors prove themselves worthy of becoming permanent, tenured faculty. Typically, pressure to publish is greatest for assistant professors. Pressure to publish increases again if an associate professor wishes to be considered for a promotion to full professorship.

Some faculty members eventually rise to the position of *department chair,* where they govern the affairs of an entire forensic science, chemistry, biology, engineering, or other academic department. Department chairs, faculty, and other professional staff members are aided in their myriad duties by *graduate assistants,* who may help develop teaching materials, moderate computer laboratories, conduct research, give examinations, teach lower-level courses, and carry out other activities.

REQUIREMENTS

High School
To prepare for a career in education, follow your school's college preparatory program and take advanced courses in English, mathematics, physical and natural science, history, and government. Composition, journalism, and communications classes are also important for developing your writing and speaking skills. You should, of course, take any forensic science courses that are offered. Many high schools are adding Introduction to Forensic Science courses in response to student and industry demand.

Postsecondary Training
As a high school teacher, you will teach not just forensic science, but classes in a variety of other areas such as math and science. If you want to teach at the high school level, you may choose to major in your subject area while taking required education courses, or you may major in secondary education with a concentration in your subject area. You will also need to student teach in an actual classroom environment.

For prospective professors, you will need at least one advanced degree in your chosen field of study, such as forensic science, chemistry, biology, or engineering. The master's degree is considered the minimum standard, and graduate work beyond the master's is usually desirable. If you hope to advance in academic rank above instructor, most institutions require a doctorate. Your graduate school program will be similar to a life of teaching—in addition to attending seminars, you'll research, prepare articles for publication, and teach some undergraduate courses. Those who teach forensic pathology, odontology, or psychiatry need to earn a medical degree.

Certification or Licensing

The American Board for Certification of Teacher Excellence offers certification for career changers—people who work in non-education-related fields who quickly want to become teachers. Contact the board for more information.

Secondary teachers who work in public schools must be licensed under regulations established by the state in which they are teaching. If moving, teachers have to comply with any other regulations in their new state to be able to teach, though many states have reciprocity agreements that make it easier for teachers to change locations.

Licensure examinations test prospective teachers for competency in basic subjects such as mathematics, reading, writing, teaching, and other subject matter proficiency. In addition, many states are moving towards a performance-based evaluation for licensing. In this case, after passing the teaching examination, prospective teachers are given provisional licenses. Only after proving themselves capable in the classroom are they eligible for a full license.

Another growing trend spurred by recent teacher shortages in high schools is alternative licensure arrangements. For those who have a bachelor's degree but lack formal education courses and training in the classroom, states can issue a provisional license. These workers immediately begin teaching under the supervision of a licensed educator for one to two years and take education classes outside of their working hours. Once they have completed the required coursework and gained experience in the classroom, they are granted a full license.

Forensic science educators typically receive certification in their area of specialty, such as fire investigation, forensic anthropology, computer forensics, questioned document examination, or forensic odontology.

Other Requirements

Many consider the desire to teach a calling. This calling is based on a love of learning. Teachers of teens and young adults must respect their students as individuals, with personalities, strengths, and weaknesses of their own. They must also be patient and self-disciplined to manage a large group independently. Because they work with students who are at very impressionable ages, they should serve as good role models. Secondary teachers should also be well organized, as you'll have to keep track of the work and progress of a number of different students.

If you aim to teach at the college level, you should enjoy reading, writing, and researching. Not only will you spend many years studying in school, but your whole career will be based on communicating your thoughts and ideas. People skills are important because you'll be dealing directly with students, administrators, and other faculty members on a daily basis. You should feel comfortable in a role of authority and possess self-confidence.

Forensic science educators should have a comprehensive knowledge of their specialty and be able to impart this knowledge and the excitement of career opportunities in forensic science to their students.

EXPLORING

To explore a teaching career, look for leadership opportunities that involve working with children. You might find summer work as a counselor in a summer camp, as a leader of a scout troop, or as an assistant in a public park or community center. To get some first-hand teaching experience, volunteer for a peer tutoring program. Many other teaching opportunities may exist in your community.

If you are interested in becoming a college professor, spend some time on a college campus to get a sense of the environment. Write to colleges for their admissions brochures and course catalogs (or check them out online); read about forensic science faculty members and the courses they teach. Before visiting college campuses, make arrangements to speak to professors who teach courses that interest you. These professors may allow you to sit in on their classes and observe.

You should also participate in science clubs and activities, which will introduce you to basic scientific concepts and investigative techniques. You can also read books and magazines about forensic science. Here are a few suggestions: *Opportunities in Forensic Science Careers,* 2nd ed., by Blythe Camenson; *Forensic Science for High School Students,* by John Funkhouser; *Fundamentals of Forensic Science,* by Max M. Houck and Jay A. Siegel; and *Crime Scene: The Ultimate Guide to Forensic Science,* by Richard Platt.

Finally, talk to your forensic science teacher about his or her career. You can also ask your teachers or school counselor to arrange an information interview with a college forensic science teacher. (You can also do this on your own; contact information for forensic science professors is available at their college's Web sites.) Questions to ask include the following: How did you prepare for this field? What do you like most and least about your career? What advice would you give to young people who want to become forensic scientists and/or forensic educators? What areas of forensic science have the most promising employment outlooks?

EMPLOYERS

Forensic science educators are employed at high schools and two- and four-year colleges throughout the United States. Some forensic science educators also work for laboratories or law enforcement agencies that require their employees to participate in continuing education.

STARTING OUT

Secondary school teachers can use their college career services offices and state departments of education to find job openings. Many local schools advertise teaching positions in newspapers. Another option is to directly contact the administration in the schools in which you'd like to work. While looking for a full-time position, you can work as a substitute teacher. In more urban areas with many schools, you may be able to find full-time substitute work.

Most forensic science educators at the college level typically work in a forensic science specialty for several years before gaining enough experience to teach others about their profession. Others may combine work as an adjunct professor with employment as a forensic scientist. Prospective college professors should start the process of finding a teaching position while in graduate school. You will need to develop a curriculum vitae (a detailed, academic resume), work on your academic writing, assist with research, attend conferences, and gain teaching experience and recommendations. Because of the competition for tenure-track positions, you may have to work for a few years in temporary positions. Some professional associations maintain lists of teaching opportunities in their areas. They may also make lists of applicants available to college administrators looking to fill an available position.

The American Academy of Forensic Sciences provides a list of colleges and universities that offer programs in forensic science at its Web site, http://www.aafs.org. This list will provide you with a starting point to explore potential career opportunities in forensic science education.

The Chronicle of Higher Education is a weekly resource that covers developments in the education industry. It offers a comprehensive list of job openings for college professors in its print and online (http://chronicle.com/jobs) editions.

ADVANCEMENT

As secondary teachers acquire experience or additional education, they can expect higher wages and more responsibilities. Teachers with leadership skills and an interest in administrative work may advance to serve as principals or supervisors, though the number of these positions is limited and competition is fierce. Another move may be into higher education, teaching education classes at a college or university. For most of these positions, additional education is required. Other common career transitions are into related fields. With additional preparation, teachers can become librarians, reading specialists, or counselors. Some forensic science teachers leave the profession to work as forensic scientists.

At the college level, the normal pattern of advancement is from instructor to assistant professor, to associate professor, to full professor. All four academic ranks are concerned primarily with teaching and research. College faculty members who have an interest in and a talent for administration may be advanced to chair of a forensic science or other department or to dean of their college. A few become college or university presidents or other types of administrators.

EARNINGS

There is no specific earnings information available for high school forensic science educators. The U.S. Department of Labor (DoL) does provide information on salaries for all high school teachers (including forensic science educators). According to the DoL, the median annual salary for secondary school teachers was $51,180 in 2008. Salaries ranged from less than $34,280 to $80,970 or more. Depending on the state, teachers usually receive a retirement plan, sick leave, and health and life insurance. Some systems grant teachers sabbatical leave.

College professors' earnings vary depending on their academic department, the size of the school, the type of school (public, private, women's only), and by the level of position the professor holds. Forensic science faculty are found in many disciplines—ranging from engineering and chemistry to biology and nursing. The U.S. Department of Labor reports that college professors earned the following mean annual salaries by academic discipline: anthropology and archeology, $73,410; biological science, $83,270; chemistry, $76,310; computer science, $74,050; criminal justice and law enforcement, $59,830; engineering, $90,070; health specialties, $102,000; law, $101,170; mathematical science, $68,130; nursing: $62,660; physics, $81,880; and psychology, $69,560. According to the DoL, in 2008 the median salary for postsecondary instructors (not otherwise classified) was

$61,360, with 10 percent earning $123,430 or more and 10 percent earning $33,950 or less. Many professors try to increase their earnings by completing research, publishing in their field, or teaching additional courses. Benefits for full-time faculty typically include health insurance and retirement funds and, in some cases, stipends for travel related to research, housing allowances, and tuition waivers for dependents.

WORK ENVIRONMENT

Most forensic science educators are contracted to work 10 months out of the year, with a two-month vacation during the summer. During their summer break, many continue their education to renew or upgrade their teaching licenses (secondary school teachers) and earn higher salaries. Teachers in schools that operate year-round work eight-week sessions with one-week breaks in between and a five-week vacation in the winter.

Forensic science teachers work in generally pleasant conditions, although some older schools may have poor heating or electrical systems. The work can seem confining, requiring them to remain in the classroom throughout most of the day. They spend some of the time in laboratories, and may be exposed to noxious chemicals or other dangerous substances, and use a variety of protective equipment to ensure their safety.

High school hours are generally 8 A.M. to 3 P.M., but teachers work more than 40 hours a week teaching, preparing for classes, grading papers, and directing extracurricular activities. Similarly, most college forensic science teachers work more than 40 hours each week. Although they may teach only two or three classes a semester, they spend many hours preparing for lectures, examining student work, and conducting research.

OUTLOOK

Employment for forensic science technicians is expected to grow much faster than the average for all careers through 2016, according to the U.S. Department of Labor. This suggests that opportunities should also be good for forensic science educators—especially college professors—since teachers will be needed to train workers for this rapidly expanding field. Forensic science educators with advanced education and experience as forensic scientists will have the best employment prospects.

Overall employment for high school teachers is expected to grow as fast as the average for all occupations through 2016. The need to replace retiring teachers will provide many opportunities nation-wide. Employment for college professors is expected to grow much faster than the average for all careers during this same time span. However, competition for full-time, tenure-track positions at four-year schools will be very strong.

FOR MORE INFORMATION

For information on forensic careers and education, contact
American Academy of Forensic Sciences
410 North 21st Street
Colorado Springs, CO 80904-2712
Tel: 719-636-1100
http://www.aafs.org

Contact the association for information about earnings and union membership for college professors.
American Association of University Professors
1133 Nineteenth Street, NW, Suite 200
Washington, DC 20036-3655
Tel: 202-737-5900
Email: aaup@aaup.org
http://www.aaup.org

This nonprofit organization "recruits, prepares, certifies and supports dedicated professionals to improve student achievement through quality teaching." Visit its Web site for information on certification and tips on finding a job.
American Board for Certification of Teacher Excellence
1225 19th Street, NW, Suite 400
Washington, DC 20036-2457
Tel: 877-669-2228
http://www.abcte.org

The AFT is a professional membership organization for teachers at all levels. In addition to membership benefits, the federation offers information on important issues affecting educators, salary surveys, and useful periodicals.
American Federation of Teachers (AFT)
555 New Jersey Avenue, NW
Washington, DC 20001-2029
Tel: 202-879-4400
http://www.aft.org

For information on colleges and universities that offer forensic science programs, contact
Council on Forensic Science Education
http://www.criminology.fsu.edu/COFSE/default.html

For information on career paths, contact
Forensic Sciences Foundation
410 North 21st Street
Colorado Springs, CO 80904-2712
Tel: 719-636-1100
http://www.forensicsciencesfoundation.org/career_paths/
   careers.htm

Visit the council's Web site to read the following resources: "What is the benefit of attending an NCATE-accredited college of education?" and "I want to be a teacher, but cannot afford college tuition. How do I get a loan, grant, or scholarship to a college?"
National Council for Accreditation of Teacher Education
   (NCATE)
2010 Massachusetts Avenue, NW, Suite 500
Washington, DC 20036-1023
Tel: 202-466-7496
Email: ncate@ncate.org
http://www.ncate.org

Forensic Science Laboratory Managers

OVERVIEW

Forensic science laboratory managers direct the operation of private and government crime laboratories. They are also known as *crime lab managers, forensic science laboratory directors,* and *crime lab directors.* There are approximately 400 private- and government-run crime labs in the United States.

HISTORY

Throughout the late 19th century, new forensic investigative methods, tests, and scientific equipment were developed. As the number of forensic science professionals grew and the science involved became more complex, demand emerged for formalized settings where evidence could be studied. In 1910 the first police crime laboratory in the world was founded at the University of Lyons in France by Dr. Edmund Locard, a professor of forensic medicine and industry pioneer. In 1923 the first forensic laboratory in the U.S. was founded by police chief August Vollmer in Los Angeles, California. In 1932 the Federal Bureau of Investigation crime lab was created.

In 1973 the American Society of Crime Laboratory Directors was founded by a small group of crime lab directors from around the United States. Today, it continues to represent the professional interests of crime laboratory managers.

Forensic science laboratory managers must have excellent communication skills in order to effectively explain laboratory findings to the media and the public. *(Pat Roque, AP Photo)*

THE JOB

Forensic science laboratory managers organize and manage personnel, equipment, support staff, and investigative departments at crime labs. They hire and supervise personnel, handle budgets, manage information systems and other technology, serve as spokespeople to the media, and are responsible for the integrity of forensic science personnel and the accuracy of the tests that they conduct. In some forensic science labs, many of these duties are delegated to assistants or to various unit heads. These assistants may supervise operations in areas such as questioned documents, fingerprint analysis, trace evidence, forensic biology, crime scene investigation, and pathology.

Forensic science laboratory managers meet regularly with their staffs to discuss cases and investigative techniques, and to address problems. Managers may organize training programs for forensic scientists and technicians. They are responsible for hiring and firing workers and conducting employee reviews.

Laboratory managers may oversee one lab or several in multiple locations. Some lab managers may continue to take an active role in investigations, gathering evidence at crime scenes, analyzing it back at the laboratory, and writing reports or testifying about their findings in courtrooms and other legal settings.

Forensic science laboratory managers have both civilian and law enforcement backgrounds.

REQUIREMENTS

High School

If you are interested in a career in crime lab management, you should start preparing in high school by taking college preparatory classes. Because communication skills are important, take as many speech and writing classes as possible. Courses in business, mathematics, and computer science are also excellent choices to help you prepare for this career.

Postsecondary Training

You may only need a bachelor's degree in forensic science, chemistry, biochemistry, biology, or a related field to work at a small crime lab, but large government labs typically require directors to have at least a master's degree and often a doctorate. The American Academy of Forensic Sciences provides a list of colleges and universities that offer degrees in forensic science and administration at its Web site (http://www.aafs.org).

A few colleges and universities, such as Oklahoma State University (http://www.healthsciences.okstate.edu/forensic/mfsa.cfm), offer graduate degrees in forensic sciences administration. Typical core classes in its master's degree program include Survey of Forensic Sciences, Quality Assurance in Forensic Sciences, Ethics in Forensic Leadership, Molecular Biology or Forensic Toxicology, Forensic Pathology and Medicine, Criminalistics, Scientific Evidence, Forensic Management and Organizational Development, and Human Resources in Health Care and Public Administration. Elective courses include Forensic Examination of Questioned Documents; Historical Aspects of Questioned Documents; Scientific Writing, Research, and Presentation; Forensic Bioscience; Drug Toxicity; Advanced Criminalistics; Forensic Psychology; and Forensic Accounting and Fraud Investigation.

Forensic science laboratory managers continue to hone their skills throughout their careers by attending seminars, workshops, and educational conferences. The American Society of Crime Laboratory Directors offers a variety of continuing education classes.

Certification or Licensing

Forensic science laboratory managers typically receive certification in their area of specialty, such as computer forensics, questioned document examination, or forensic entomology.

Many managers obtain certification from the American Board of Criminalistics. Certification is available in comprehensive criminalistics, as well as in drug analysis, fire debris analysis, molecular biology, trace evidence-hairs and fibers, and trace evidence-paints and polymers. Applicants must satisfy education and experience requirements and take and pass an examination.

The American College of Forensic Examiners offers the certified forensic consultant program, which provides an overview of the U.S. judicial system. This certification would be useful for laboratory managers who are required to testify in court. Contact the college for more information.

Other Requirements

Forensic science laboratory managers must be highly ethical and ensure that their employees achieve the highest quality standards when conducting investigations and analyses. They should have excellent leadership skills, be highly organized, and have strong communication skills in order to interact successfully with workers that range from secretaries and janitors, to human resource professionals, to attorneys and law enforcement officials, to forensic scientists.

In addition, managers must be able to coordinate their facility's many related functions. They need to understand, for instance, financial operations, purchasing, organizational development, scientific departments, and other areas that they manage. They must also have the ability to make some decisions with speed and others with considerable study.

Some laboratories may require managers to be U.S. citizens or permanent residents of the United States.

EXPLORING

If you are considering a career as a forensic science laboratory manager, you should take advantage of opportunities in high school to develop some of the skills required in this line of work. Because managers need strong leadership and communication skills, participation in clubs as a leader or active member and in debate and speech clubs is helpful. You can also read books about forensic science. Ask your science teacher or school counselor to organize a tour of a crime laboratory or to arrange an information interview with a laboratory director. Visit the Web sites of crime labs to learn more about investigative techniques and typical job responsibilities. The FBI Laboratory's Web site (http://www.fbi. gov/hq/lab/labhome.htm) is an excellent place to start.

EMPLOYERS

There are approximately 400 private- and government-run crime labs in the United States. They are operated by prosecuting attorneys' offices, law enforcement agencies and other government organizations, and companies in the private sector.

STARTING OUT

No one begins their career as a forensic science laboratory manager. Since this career is the highest-level position in a forensic laboratory, it takes many years to gain enough experience and education to become qualified to lead such an important facility. Managers start their careers as entry-level technicians or scientists and gradually gain enough tenure and experience to become promoted to department manager, assistant laboratory manager, and finally, laboratory manager. Applicants for lab manager positions usually have at least five years of experience working in a crime lab, and one to two years working in a managerial position.

Forensic science job openings can also be found by contacting your university's career services office or through bulletins of state and national forensic science associations. Large professional society meetings may offer on-site notices of job openings. The American Society of Crime Laboratory Directors posts job openings for forensic professionals at its Web site (http://www.ascld. org/content/employment-opportunities).

ADVANCEMENT

Forensic science laboratory managers advance by receiving pay raises or by seeking employment at larger, more prestigious crime laboratories. Others become forensic science consultants or college professors.

EARNINGS

Salaries for forensic science laboratory managers depend on the type of facility, geographic location, the size of its staff, and its budget. There is no comprehensive salary information available for forensic science laboratory managers. The U.S. Department of Labor does provide information on managers, not otherwise classified (a category that includes crime lab managers). The median salary for these professionals was $90,230 in 2008. Salaries ranged from less than $46,700 to $153,500 or more. In 2008, managers working for the federal government earned a mean annual salary of $99,240, and those employed by state government agencies earned $75,930.

Benefits include paid vacation, health, disability, life insurance, retirement or pension plans, and sometimes use of a vehicle.

WORK ENVIRONMENT

Most forensic science laboratory managers work five days a week, but often work extra on weekends and holidays, when necessary. However, hours can be irregular because laboratories operate around the clock; emergencies may require the manager's supervision any time of the day or night. Lab managers may travel to crime scenes to collect evidence or supervise workers. They also occasionally testify in court and must participate in press conferences for major criminal cases. Some travel to other cities for professional conferences and seminars should also be expected. Forensic science laboratory managers who work on cases are exposed to crime scenes that are often grisly and disturbing, and may come in contact with hazardous chemicals and bodily fluids. They wear protective equipment to reduce the risk of injury or infection.

OUTLOOK

Employment for forensic science laboratory managers should be fair in the next decade. This is a very small field, and only the best educated and most qualified people rise to the position of laboratory director. Most job openings occur as a result of existing directors leaving the field for other positions or retirement. Those with advanced education and experience in forensic science will have the best employment prospects.

FOR MORE INFORMATION

For information on forensic careers and education, contact
American Academy of Forensic Sciences
410 North 21st Street
Colorado Springs, CO 80904-2712
Tel: 719-636-1100
http://www.aafs.org

For information on certification, contact
American Board of Criminalistics
PO Box 1123
Wausau, WI 54402-1123
http://www.criminalistics.com

Visit the society's Web site for job listings, information on scholarships for college students, answers to frequently asked questions about careers in forensic science, and industry news.
American Society of Crime Laboratory Directors
139K Technology Drive
Garner, NC 27529-7970
Tel: 919-773-2044
http://www.ascld.org

For information on employment opportunities in California, contact
California Association of Crime Laboratory Directors
http://www.cacld.net

To learn more about forensic services at the FBI, visit the FBI Laboratory Division's Web site.
Federal Bureau of Investigation (FBI)
J. Edgar Hoover Building
935 Pennsylvania Avenue, NW
Washington, DC 20535-0001
Tel: 202-324-3000
http://www.fbi.gov/hq/lab/labhome.htm

For general information about forensic science, contact
International Association for Identification
2535 Pilot Knob Road, Suite 117
Mendota Heights, MN 55120-1120
Tel: 651-681-8566
http://www.theiai.org

INTERVIEW

Dean Gialamas is the president of the American Society of Crime Lab Directors and the director of the Forensic Science Services Division for the Orange County Sheriff's Department in Orange County, California. He discussed his career and crime lab management with the editors of Careers in Focus: Forensics.

Q. What made you want to enter this career?

A. I set off for college wanting to go to medical school to become a pediatrician. While taking some chemistry courses required for my degrees, I had a professor named Dr. Vince Guinn. During his lectures he frequently would explain how chemistry was often used in real world applications and often mentioned forensic science and would explain about cases he was involved with. His most famous case was the assassination of President John F. Kennedy. He was instrumental in the bullet lead analysis of the "pristine bullet" found on the stretcher. His stories intrigued me so much that I went in to speak to him about the field and he convinced me to try an internship at a local crime lab (the one I now manage) to see if it was a good fit for me. A few months into my internship I knew this was the lifelong career choice for me.

Q. Can you tell us about the American Society of Crime Lab Directors and the Forensic Science Services Division at the Orange County Sheriff's Department?

A. The American Society of Crime Laboratory Directors (ASCLD) is a nonprofit professional organization of crime laboratory directors and forensic science managers dedicated to providing excellence in forensic science through leadership and innovation. As an organization, ASCLD provides leadership in the forensic community as well as assistance to its members by providing information, training, and networking opportunities.

The ASCLD was founded in 1973 by a small group of crime lab directors from throughout the United States to foster professional interests and to assist in the development of laboratory management principles and techniques. Today, ASCLD is composed of more than 650 crime laboratory directors and forensic science managers that represent more than 250 local, state, federal, and private crime laboratories in the United States. Membership also includes directors from 30 international laboratories, as well as national and international academic affiliates.

The Orange County Sheriff's Department's Forensic Science Services Division is a well-regarded, ASCLD/LAB ISO 17025-accredited full-service forensic laboratory, operating a $43 million dollar budget and employing more than 150 scientists, specialists, and support personnel. Housed in a state-of-the-art facility, the laboratory serves a population of more than three million residents and provides forensic services to more than 50 local, state, and federal criminal justice agencies operating within Orange County in areas including toxicology, forensic alcohol, controlled substances, firearms, document examination, DNA, trace evidence, latent fingerprint comparison and processing, crime scene investigation, and automated fingerprint identification.

Q. What are your main and secondary job duties as a crime lab director?

A. As a division commander, my main duties are to lead and manage the crime lab operation. We are an operation that provides 24/7 support, 365 days a year. I am responsible for the management of the budget, personnel, a state-of-the-art facility and providing support to both the dedicated men and women working in the laboratory as well as support to the client agencies we serve. A key component to the successful operation of the laboratory is maintaining a robust professional environment with strong and uncompromising professionalism along with a highly progressive quality management system to assure the highest quality work product for the public and the criminal justice system.

Q. What are the most important personal and professional qualities for crime lab directors?

A. The most important qualities of a forensic scientist (including laboratory director) are to have strong and uncompromising character and integrity. Evidence is a "Silent Witness." It is our job to speak on behalf of the evidence to help bring those to justice that have perpetrated crimes, help free those wrongly accused, and bring closure to victims and their families. Anyone working in this field needs to have a strong set of morals and ethics and have the honesty, fairness, and strong conviction to do the right thing all the time. Anything less, and you will be destined for failure and disgrace.

Q. What advice would you give to high school students who are interested in entering forensic science careers?

A. There are three primary areas of advice for those interested in this field. First, realize that this field has become very popular and impacted due to television shows like *CSI* and *Forensic Files*. Don't get discouraged about the difficulty in finding a job in this career. For every one position I hire, I have at least 50 qualified applicants competing for that one position.

Second, get involved in the field and expand your knowledge base. Look for internship opportunities, join professional organizations, conduct research, get an advanced or graduate degree ... all of these help make you an attractive candidate to any forensic science laboratory.

And third, remember that decisions you make at a young age can affect whether you can be employed or not. Felony or misdemeanor convictions, drug use, theft, at-fault traffic accidents, bad credit, and many other poor life choices and experiences can negatively affect your ability to work in this field. A detailed security background is required and the choices you make today can affect your career choice in the future. Every choice has consequences, so choose wisely and carefully!

Forensic Toxicologists

OVERVIEW

Toxicologists design and conduct studies to determine the potential toxicity of substances to humans, plants, and animals. *Forensic toxicologists* are specialists who detect and identify the presence of poisons or legal or illegal drugs in an individual's body.

HISTORY

The study of the effects of poisons (toxins) began in the 1500s, when doctors documented changes in body tissues of people who died after a long illness. As microscopes and other forms of scientific equipment improved, scientists were able to study in greater detail the impacts of chemicals on the human body and the causes of disease.

In 1813 Mathieu Orifila, a Spanish chemist and physician, published what many consider to be the first comprehensive book on forensic toxicology. Orifila, who is considered the father of modern toxicology, focused his work on the need for quality assurance in the field and developing a systematic approach to identifying poisons. He played a major role in the development of tests for the presence of blood in a forensic setting. Orifila also was the first scientist to try to use a microscope to study semen and blood stains. Another interesting development in the history of forensic toxicology occurred in 1836. A man was accused in court of poisoning his grandfather with coffee that was laced with arsenic. James Marsh, a Scottish chemist, was asked by the prosecution to perform the standard test for arsenic. The test came back positive, but by the time Marsh could show the test to the jury, it had deteriorated. The defendant was acquitted. Marsh was outraged by the verdict and worked to create a more effective test. He eventually developed a test that could detect even the most miniscule amount of arsenic. The test, known as the Marsh Test, is still in use today.

Today forensic toxicologists are in strong demand not only to help law enforcement officials solve crimes, but also to test sports athletes for illegal drug use, investigate the poisoning of animals, and perform toxicological-related duties in a variety of fields.

THE JOB

The best-known part of the forensic toxicologist's job is seeking to determine whether illegal or prescription drugs, poisons, metals, alcohol, gases (such as carbon dioxide), or other chemicals contributed to a person's death. In doing this, the toxicologist works with law enforcement officers, other forensic scientists, and crime scene investigators. The toxicologist performs tests on body fluid and tissue samples received from the forensic pathologist and then assists with the interpretation of the findings. Most forensic toxicology laboratories routinely screen for perhaps a few hundred to a few thousand chemical compounds. As with all the forensic sciences, proper record keeping, documentation, and quality control are emphasized.

Other forensic toxicologists help investigate crimes in which an individual's drug or alcohol use is a factor in the crime or may be a defense. This involves the same application of techniques as in a death investigation, but it usually involves lower concentrations of drugs, requiring more sensitive testing to produce precise results. Forensic toxicologists also work on cases involving the poisoning of animals, the use of drugs to facilitate sexual assault, and illicit and performance-enhancing drug use in sports, from track and field and the well-known team sports to horse and dog racing.

More and more companies are requiring their employees whose jobs involve dangerous work conditions or could impact the safety of others (such as truck drivers, airline pilots, and railroad workers) to undergo drug testing. This has meant more work for forensic toxicologists. This aspect of toxicology is usually confined to the detection of only a handful of specific drugs in a large number of urine samples; some laboratories perform tests on more than 10,000 samples a day. Testing of this type is evolving toward the use of specimens other than blood or urine, such as sweat, hair, and saliva.

While forensic toxicology is a dynamic and fascinating field, it's not all a bed of roses. Toxicologists are expected to routinely handle all types of tissues and fluids, from blood to urine to liver to brain

Books to Read

Houck, Max M., and Jay A. Siegel. *Fundamentals of Forensic Science*. St. Louis, Mo.: Academic Press, 2006.
James, Stuart H., and Jon J. Nordby. *Forensic Science: An Introduction to Scientific and Investigative Techniques*. 3d ed. Boca Raton, Fla.: CRC Press, 2009.
Kubic, Thomas. *Forensic Science Laboratory Manual and Workbook*. 2d ed. Boca Raton, Fla.: CRC Press, 2005.
Platt, Richard. *Crime Scene: The Ultimate Guide to Forensic Science*. New York: Dorling Kindersley, 2006.
Ramsland, Katherine. *Beating the Devil's Game: A History of Forensic Science and Criminal Investigation*. New York: Berkley Trade, 2008.
Saferstein, Richard. *Criminalistics: An Introduction to Forensic Science*. 9th ed. Upper Saddle River, N.J.: Prentice Hall, 2008.
Saferstein, Richard. *Forensic Science: From the Crime Scene to the Crime Lab*. Upper Saddle River, N.J.: Prentice Hall, 2008.
Williams, Judith. *Forensic Scientist: Careers Solving Crimes and Scientific Mysteries*. Berkeley Heights, N.J.: Enslow Publishers Inc., 2009.

tissue to hair. In addition, the tissues they are provided can be badly decomposed, making their job even harder. Toxicology testing of employees and athletes can be frustrating, since not only do users of illegal substances take steps to try to avoid detection, but there are millions of chemicals for which no testing has ever been developed. Finally, as with other careers in forensic science, the forensic toxicologist must be able to describe his or her working methods and findings and explain their meaning in a straightforward manner for judges, juries, and lawyers when necessary.

REQUIREMENTS
High School
While in high school, you can best prepare for a career as a forensic toxicologist by taking courses in both the physical and biological sciences (chemistry and biology, for example), algebra and geometry, and physics. English and other courses that improve written and verbal communication skills will also be useful, since forensic toxicologists must write and report on complicated study results. Any courses that provide an introduction to forensic science will also be helpful.

Postsecondary Training

Most forensic toxicologists obtain their undergraduate degrees in one of the physical sciences, and take coursework primarily in pharmacology and chemistry, but also study mathematics (including mathematical modeling), biology, chemistry, statistics, biochemistry, pathology, anatomy, and research methods.

Career opportunities for graduates with bachelor's degrees are limited; the majority of forensic toxicologists go on to obtain master's or doctorate degrees in toxicology with a specialization in forensic science or forensic toxicology. Graduate programs vary depending on one's field of study, but forensic toxicology programs may include courses such as forensic medicine, forensic toxicology, scientific evidence and statistics, environmental toxicology, and toxic substances. Doctorate programs generally last four to five years. The American Academy of Forensic Sciences provides a list of colleges that offer forensic toxicology programs at its Web site (http://www.aafs.org).

Certification or Licensing

Certification recognizes an individual's competence and expertise in toxicology and the specialty of forensic toxicology and can enhance career opportunities. The American Board of Toxicology certifies toxicologists after they pass a comprehensive examination and complete the necessary educational requirements. Contact the board for details.

Certification can also be obtained from the American Board of Forensic Toxicology. Those who are seeking certification as a diplomate of the board or certification as a forensic toxicology specialist must meet professional experience and educational requirements, and pass an examination. Contact the board for more information.

The American Board of Clinical Chemistry (http://www.abclinchem.org) also offers certification to forensic toxicologists.

Other Requirements

Toxicologists must be hard workers and be dedicated to their field of study. They should be ethical, good communicators, and highly organized. To succeed in their work, they must be careful observers and have an eye for detail. The ability to work both alone and as part of a team is also needed for research.

Those who wish to pursue this career must be skilled in analytic chemistry techniques, and it helps to have an inquisitive nature—the job often involves the solving of puzzles.

Because of the nature of their work, forensic toxicologists must also realize the potential dangers of working with hazardous materials.

EXPLORING

If you are interested in pursuing a career as a forensic toxicologist, consider joining a science club in addition to taking biology and chemistry courses to further develop your laboratory skills. A career counselor or science teacher might be able to help you arrange a discussion with a practicing forensic toxicologist to explore career options. Part-time jobs in research laboratories or hospitals are an excellent way to explore science firsthand, although opportunities may be limited and require higher levels of education and experience.

EMPLOYERS

Forensic toxicologists work in laboratories for law-enforcement agencies, medical-examiner departments, and companies that perform workplace drug testing. They may also work for agencies that monitor drug use in sports, hospitals, and colleges and universities. At colleges and universities they work as professors in toxicology, chemistry, pathology, and pharmacology departments.

STARTING OUT

Those with the necessary education and experience should contact the appropriate research departments in hospitals, colleges and universities, government agencies, or private businesses. Often, school professors and career services advisers provide job leads and recommendations.

Networking with professionals is another useful way to enter the field. Past work with a team of toxicologists or forensic toxicologists during graduate study may open doors to future research opportunities. Membership in a professional society can also offer more networking contacts. The Society of Toxicology and the American College of Medical Toxicology both offer job placement assistance to members. Many professional associations, such as the Society of Forensic Toxicologists (http://www.soft-tox.org), offer job listings at their Web sites.

Some people enter the field after having successful careers in pharmacology, pharmacokinetics, clinical chemistry, or medicinal chemistry.

ADVANCEMENT

Skilled forensic toxicologists will find many advancement opportunities, although specific promotions depend on the size and type of organization where the forensic toxicologist is employed. Those working for private companies may become heads of research departments.

Because of their involvement in developing important company policy, highly skilled and respected toxicologists may become vice presidents or presidents of companies. Obviously, this type of promotion would entail a change in job responsibilities, involving more administrative tasks than research activities.

Forensic toxicologists working for educational institutions may become professors, heads of a department, or deans. Forensic toxicologists who want to continue to research and teach can advance to positions with higher pay and increased job responsibilities. Those working at universities usually write grant proposals, teach courses, and train graduate students. University positions often do not pay as well as industrial positions, but they offer more independence in pursuing research interests.

EARNINGS

As trained professionals, toxicologists have good earning potential. Wages vary depending on level of experience, education, and employer. According to the Society of Toxicology, entry-level toxicologists with a Ph.D. earn $35,000 to $60,000. With a Ph.D. and 10 years of experience, toxicologists can earn between $70,000 and $100,000 a year. Toxicologists in executive positions earn more than $100,000, and in the corporate arena they can earn more than $200,000. Those in private industry earn slightly more than those in government or academic positions.

Toxicologists are often categorized under the specialty of analytical chemistry. The U.S. Department of Labor reports that the median annual salary for chemists in 2008 was $66,230. Salaries ranged from less than $37,840 to $113,080 or more.

Salaries for toxicologists in all fields are, in general, on the rise, but the society reports that the biggest factor determining earning potential is not location but type of employer. Certification also plays a large role in salary level; forensic toxicologists who are certified earn higher salaries than those who have not earned certification. Comparing gender differences, the society found that women continue to be paid less than their male counterparts.

Forensic toxicologists who work for a company or government agency usually receive benefits such as vacation days, sick leave, health and life insurance, and a savings and pension program. Self-employed toxicologists must provide their own benefits.

WORK ENVIRONMENT

Toxicologists usually work in well-equipped laboratories or offices, either as part of a team or alone. Research in libraries or in the field is a major part of the job. Some toxicologists work a standard 40-hour workweek, although many work longer hours. Overtime should be expected if an important assignment is on deadline. Research and testing can be both physically and mentally tiring, with much of the laboratory work and analysis done while under time restrictions. Some travel may be required to testify at hearings, to collect field samples, or to attend professional conferences.

Because their work involves studying the impact of toxic material, toxicologists must be willing to handle contaminated material and adhere to the strict safety precautions required.

OUTLOOK

Employment opportunities for toxicologists are expected to continue to be good. Workplace drug testing and the testing of athletes and animals involved in professional sports are expected to increase in coming years. There will also be continuing opportunities with law enforcement agencies. Forensic toxicologists with advanced training and experience will have the best employment prospects.

FOR MORE INFORMATION

For information on forensic careers, education, and its membership section for toxicologists, contact
American Academy of Forensic Sciences
410 North 21st Street
Colorado Springs, CO 80904-2712
Tel: 719-636-1100
http://www.aafs.org

For information on certification, contact
American Board of Forensic Toxicology
410 North 21st Street
Colorado Springs, CO 80904-2712
Tel: 719-636-1100
http://www.abft.org

For certification information, contact
American Board of Toxicology
PO Box 30054
Raleigh, NC 27622-0054
Tel: 919-841-5022
Email: info@abtox.org
http://www.abtox.org

For information on educational programs and other toxicology resources, contact
American College of Medical Toxicology
10645 North Tatum Boulevard, Suite 200-111
Phoenix, AZ 85028-3068
Tel: 623-533-6340
http://www.acmt.net

For more information about the field, contact
International Association of Forensic Toxicologists
Email: info@tiaft.org
http://www.tiaft.org

For information on forensic toxicology and career options in the field, contact
Society of Forensic Toxicologists
One MacDonald Center
1 North MacDonald Street, Suite 15
Mesa, AZ 85201-7340
http://www.soft-tox.org

For general career information, contact
Society of Toxicology
1821 Michael Faraday Drive, Suite 300
Reston, VA 20190-5348
Tel: 703-438-3115
Email: sothq@toxicology.org
http://www.toxicology.org

Questioned Document Examiners

OVERVIEW

Questioned document examiners study a wide variety of documents to determine if they are authentic or if they have been altered in any manner. They are also known as *forensic document examiners* and *handwriting* and *typewriting identification experts*.

HISTORY

The authenticity of documents and handwriting has been questioned and analyzed for thousands of years. Early methods of analysis were largely unscientific, which often resulted in erroneous findings by the document examiner. It wasn't until 1609 that the Frenchman François Demelle published the first discourse on systematic document examination. The first recorded use of questioned document analysis occurred in Germany in 1810, according to the Forensic Science Timeline (http://www.forensicdna.com/Timeline020702.pdf), a Web site maintained by Norah Rudin and Keith Inman.

Albert S. Osborn is considered to be the father of questioned document examination in the United States. His *Questioned Documents* (1910) and *The Problem of Proof* (1922) are credited with fueling the development of questioned document examination as a respected scientific field. Starting in 1913 Osborn met with other document examiners to discuss issues in the field. These conversations continued informally for parts of four decades until 1942, when Osborn and his colleagues formed the American Society of Questioned Document Examiners. He became

QUICK FACTS

School Subjects
Computer science
Mathematics

Personal Skills
Communication/ideas
Technical/scientific

Work Environment
Primarily indoors
One location with some
  travel

Minimum Education Level
Bachelor's degree

Salary Range
$30,990 to $49,860 to
  $80,330+

Certification or Licensing
Recommended

Outlook
Faster than the average

DOT
N/A

GOE
04.03.02

NOC
N/A

O*NET-SOC
19-4092.00

the organization's first president, and the organization continues to be a leading advocate for questioned document examiners today.

THE JOB

A questioned document examiner works in an office or a laboratory, examining documents to determine if they are authentic and/or to discover who wrote them. The examination of documents is important in the fight against many types of white-collar crime, including forgery, counterfeiting, fraud, and the enormous and still-growing problem of identity theft. The examiner may be called on to present expert testimony in court to demonstrate the basis and reasons for his/her opinion.

Most of an examiner's work involves some form of handwriting problem, and therefore the field is sometimes referred to as handwriting identification and the practitioner as a handwriting expert. The examiner should have excellent eyesight, but even so a magnifying glass or microscope is often used to analyze noteworthy characteristics of a person's handwriting, compare those characteristics to a known standard writing sample, and evaluate the similarities and differences between the two to arrive at a conclusion as to the authenticity of the disputed writing.

Other questioned document examiners specialize in the identification of types of instruments used to produce a document, from writing tools (pens and pencils) to machines such as inkjet and laser printers, fax machines, and typewriters. Typewriters, for example, can be identified by noting their typeface design and whether they are manual or electric or have a fabric ribbon or carbon film ribbon. The examiner also considers that machines display specific individual characteristics after years of wear and tear and any incidents of damage. Other items to be examined may include inks (writing, printing, stamp pad, ink jet and typewriter), toners, pencil marks, erasure residues, correction material, and paper.

Another important part of the questioned document examiner's work is to detect whether a portion of a document has been altered, whether text has been added, or whether some portion has been rendered not easily visible. If information has been removed or altered, then the method is determined and described, and if possible the text of the obliterated entry is deciphered. An imaging instrument called a Video Spectral Comparator (VSC) is often used in such cases. Using ultraviolet radiation, the VSC can be used to reconstruct shredded documents or to confirm discrepancies between parts of a document, which may reveal, for example, that a page has been added to a contract.

A questioned document examiner works to verify the signature of a state Senate candidate on candidate qualification papers. Questions had arisen regarding the authenticity of the signature. The examiner determined that the signature was a forgery. *(Phil Coale, AP Photo)*

Document examiners are also often called on to identify and decipher indented writing, which is an imprint that may be left on underlying pages when a top sheet of paper is written upon. This writing impression is a product of the pressure of the writing utensil and the thickness of the paper. Indented writing can be very useful as a form of connecting evidence, such as establishing a link between a robbery note and a writing pad recovered from a suspect. An instrument known as an Electrostatic Detection Apparatus is used to produce a viewable image of the indented writing on transparent film.

Questioned document examiners use a variety of tools to analyze documents and handwriting, including microscopes, magnifiers, lighting instruments, projectors, photographic equipment, electrostatic detection apparatus, ultraviolet and infrared light outfits, video spectral equipment, and other instruments.

Although most questioned document examiners are civilian workers, some are sworn law enforcement officers.

REQUIREMENTS

High School
In high school, take as many science classes as possible, as well as classes in mathematics and computer science. English and speech classes will help you to develop your communication skills, which you will use to write reports, interact with coworkers, and testify in court.

Postsecondary Training
There are no college degree programs in questioned document examination. Colleges do offer coursework in this field as part of forensic science, criminal justice, or criminalistics degree programs. The American Academy of Forensic Sciences offers a list of colleges and universities that offer certificates and degrees in forensic science and related fields at its Web site (http://www.aafs.org).

Questioned document examiners typically have a bachelor's degree in one of the sciences, such as chemistry or forensic science, and obtain their skills by participating in a two- to four-year apprenticeship program at a forensic science laboratory or with an examiner in private practice. The instructor should be a member of the American Board of Forensic Document Examiners, the American Society of Questioned Document Examiners, or the Questioned Documents Section of the American Academy of Forensic Sciences.

Questioned document examiners continue to hone their skills throughout their careers by attending seminars, workshops, and educational conferences.

Certification or Licensing
The American Board of Forensic Document Examiners provides voluntary certification to questioned document examiners. Applicants must have completed a two-year apprenticeship, have a bachelor's degree, and be working full time in the field. Certification is often required by federal and state crime laboratories.

The Fraud Museum

If you live near Austin, Texas, or plan to take a vacation there with your parents, you can visit the Association of Certified Fraud Examiners Fraud Museum, which contains documents from some of the most famous and obscure financial frauds in history. Some of the documents you can view at the museum include:

- French letter (1876) (An individual in Belfort to Tournus, France, tried to mail this letter using a previously used stamp. The French postal authorities caught on to this ruse before the letter could be mailed.)
- Photograph of Clarence Hatry & Associates (1929) (Their fraudulent activities played a major role in the stock market crash of 1929.)
- Check signed by Ivan Boesky (1975) (This stockbroker became "synonymous with insider trading on Wall Street." Boesky received a 3.5-year prison sentence and a fine of $100 million as punishment for his illegal activities.)
- Enron Corporation stock certificate (2002) (This certificate is from the energy giant Enron, which collapsed in 2002 as a result of fraud of more than $30 billion. The stock became worthless and tens of thousands of workers lost their jobs.)

The museum is open from 8:00 A.M. to 5 P.M. daily except on major holidays. It is located at the following address: The Gregor Building, 716 West Avenue, Austin, TX 78701-2727. If you can't make it to Austin, visit http://www.acfe.com/documents/fraud-museum.pdf for an interesting overview of some of the exhibits in the museum.

Other Requirements

Questioned document examiners must have good communication, organizational, and observational skills. They must also have good eyesight, have excellent communication skills, and be able to work independently. It is extremely important that document examiners be highly ethical in their work.

EXPLORING

There are many ways to learn more about forensic document examination. For example, you can ask your teacher or counselor to arrange an information interview with a professional in the field or schedule a tour of a crime laboratory in your area. You can also visit the Web sites of professional associations (see For More Information at the end of this article) for answers to frequently asked questions about the field. Finally, you can read books and magazines about forensic science and questioned document examination. Here are a few suggestions: *Forensic Document Examination: Principles and Practice,* by Katherine M. Koppenhaver; *Forensic Document Examination Techniques,* by Thomas W. Vastrick; and *Detecting Forgery: Forensic Investigation of Documents,* by Joe Nickell.

EMPLOYERS

Many large police organizations, as well as most state and federal law enforcement agencies, employ questioned document examiners. Others work in the private sector for insurance companies, law firms, and other organizations. A growing number of forensic document examiners work independently as consultants.

STARTING OUT

Most employers require applicants to have a bachelor's degree and have completed an apprenticeship with an experienced questioned document examiner. Law enforcement agencies typically post job listings and requirements at their Web sites. Job listings are also available at the Web sites of the Southeastern Association of Forensic Document Examiners (http://www.safde.org/careers.htm) and the American Board of Forensic Document Examiners (http://www.abfde.org/Jobs.html).

ADVANCEMENT

Questioned document examiners who are civilian employees can advance by receiving higher wages, working for large agencies, or by being assigned managerial responsibilities. Some advance by opening their own consulting firms or by becoming college professors.

Law enforcement officers advance by rising through the ranks (sergeant, captain, and so on), receiving pay raises, or by leaving law enforcement and becoming educators or private consultants.

EARNINGS

There is no comprehensive salary information available for questioned document examiners, but the U.S. Department of Labor (DoL) provides information on earnings for forensic science technicians (a category that includes technicians who specialize in handwriting analysis). The DoL reports that the median salary for forensic science technicians was $49,860 in 2008. Salaries ranged from less than $30,990 to $80,330 or more. Forensic science technicians employed by local government agencies earned mean annual salaries of $53,300, and those employed by state agencies earned $51,910.

Questioned document examiners who work as consultants may be paid by the hour, by the day, or via a flat fee that covers specific tasks required for a particular case.

Benefits for document examiners depend on the employer; however, they usually include such items as health insurance, retirement or 401(k) plans, and paid vacation days. Self-employed workers must provide their own benefits.

WORK ENVIRONMENT

Questioned document examiners spend most of their time working in clean, well-lit crime laboratories. They may travel to crime scenes to gather evidence and to courthouses to participate in depositions or testify regarding their findings. Questioned document examiners typically work a standard 40-hour week, but may need to work overtime if an investigation is on a tight deadline.

OUTLOOK

The U.S. Department of Labor predicts that employment for forensic science technicians (a category that includes technicians who specialize in handwriting analysis) will grow much faster than the average for all occupations through 2016. There should be many opportunities for document examiners as computers and other types of technology allow criminals to create more sophisticated forgeries. Funding deficits at government laboratories may reduce employment opportunities for questioned document examiners. As a result, opportunities may be better in the private sector.

FOR MORE INFORMATION

For information on forensic careers, education, and its membership section for questioned document examiners, contact
   American Academy of Forensic Sciences
   410 North 21st Street
   Colorado Springs, CO 80904-2712
   Tel: 719-636-1100
   http://www.aafs.org

For information on certification, contact
American Board of Forensic Document Examiners
http://www.abfde.org

For more information on forensic document examination, contact
American Society of Questioned Document Examiners
PO Box 18298
Long Beach, CA 90807-8298
http://www.asqde.org

For industry information, contact
International Association for Identification
2535 Pilot Knob Road, Suite 117
Mendota Heights, MN 55120-1120
Tel: 651-681-8566
http://www.theiai.org

For more information about the field, contact the following organizations:
Southeastern Association of Forensic Document Examiners
http://www.safde.org/whatwedo.htm

Southwestern Association of Forensic Document Examiners
http://www.swafde.org

Index

Entries and page numbers in **bold** indicate major treatment of a topic.

A

AAMC. *See* Association of American Medical Colleges (AAMC)
accountants. *See* forensic accountants and auditors
Accreditation Board for Engineering and Technology 101
ACS. *See* American Chemical Society (ACS)
Addington, Anthony 86
Advancement section, explained 3
AICPA. *See* American Institute of Certified Public Accountants (AICPA)
American Academy of Forensic Sciences
   computer forensics specialists 8
   crime scene investigators 19
   criminalists 27, 28
   fingerprint analysts 38
   forensic biologists 73
   forensic chemists 89
   forensic odontologists 129, 135
   forensic pathologists 145
   forensic science educators 166
   forensic science laboratory managers 173
   forensic toxicologists 184
   questioned documents examiners 192
   Questioned Documents Section 192
American Academy of Psychiatry and the Law 149, 152, 153
American Airlines Flight 191 127
American Anthropological Association 67
American Association of Certified Fraud Examiners Fraud Museum 193
American Association of Engineering Societies 103
American Association of Nurses 117
American Association of Physical Anthropologists 65, 67
American Board for Certification of Teacher Excellence 164
American Board of Clinical Chemistry 184
American Board of Criminalistics 27
American Board of Forensic Anthropology 65
American Board of Forensic Document Examiners 192, 194
American Board of Forensic Entomology 112
American Board of Forensic Odontology 133
American Board of Forensic Psychology 152–153
American Board of Forensic Toxicology 184
American Board of Pathology 140
American Board of Professional Psychology 152–153
American Board of Psychiatry and Neurology 153
American Board of Toxicology 184
American Chemical Society (ACS) 89
American College of Forensic Examiners
   computer forensics specialists 9
   criminalists 27

fingerprint analysts 39
forensic biologists 73
forensic botanists 82
forensic chemists 89
forensic odontologists 129
American College of Medicine 185
American Dental Association
   Commission on Dental Accreditation 129
   Council on Dental Education and Licensure 128
   forensic odontologists 128–129, 131
American Entomological Society 112–113
American Institute of Certified Public Accountants (AICPA) 55–56, 60
The American Journal of Forensic Medicine and Pathology 162
American Legal Nurse Consultant Certification Board 120
American Nurse Credentialing Center 120
American Nursing Association 121
American Psychiatric Association 152, 153
American Psychological Association 148, 153
American Psychology-Law Society 154
American Society of Crime Laboratory Directors 171, 173, 175, 177–180
American Society of Forensic Odontology (ASFO) 133, 135
American Society of Plant Biologists 83
American Society of Questioned Document Examiners 189, 192
Armed Forces Institute of Pathology 133
Arthur Andersen 60
ASCLD. *See* American Society of Crime Laboratory Directors
ASFO. *See* American Society of Forensic Odontology (ASFO)
Association of American Medical Colleges (AAMC) 152
Association of Certified Fraud Examiners 56
Association of Firearm and Tool Mark Examiners 27
auditors. *See* forensic accountants and auditors
Austin, Thomas 137
Automated Fingerprint Identification Systems (Komarinski) 39
Avery, Oswald 71

B

Bertino, Anthony J. 28
Biological Resources Discipline 83
biologists 70. *See also* forensic biologists
Blandy, Mary 86
Boesky, Ivan 193
Botanical Society of America (BSA) 80, 82, 85
botanists 79. *See also* forensic botanists
Bowdoin College 62
Britz, Marjie T. 9
Brown v. the Board of Education 148
BSA. *See* Botanical Society of America (BSA)
Bureau of Legal Dentistry 130

C

Caldwell, Harry H. 16
California, University of at Berkeley 160
California Criminalistics Institute (CCI) 96
Camenson, Blythe 165
Carlow University 55
Central Intelligence Agency 28
certified fraud examiners. *See* forensic accountants and auditors
Charles (Duke of Burgundy) 125
chemists 86. *See also* forensic chemists
Chernobyl nuclear disaster (Soviet Union) 102
The Chronicle of Higher Education 166
Civil Service Commission (New York) 36
Clarence Henry & Associates 193
Clinical Atlas of Variations of the Bones of the Hands and Feet (Dwight) 62
clinical forensic pathologists 139
Coale, Phil 191
Cobb, Cathy 90
Components Failure Museum (Web site) 102
Computer Analysis and Response Team of FBI 5
computer examiners. *See* computer forensics specialists
Computer Forensics and Cyber Crime: An Introduction (Britz) 9
Computer Forensics For Dummies (Volonino) 9
Computer Forensics: Incident Response Essentials (Kruse and Heiser) 9–10, 12
computer forensics specialists 5–14
  advancement 10
  certification or licensing 9
  computer security specialists 10
  earnings 11
  educational requirements 8
  employers 10
  employment outlook 11
  exploring the field 9
  high school requirements 8
  history 5–6
  information 11–12
  interview 12–14
  job, described 6–8
  organizations 6, 8, 10
  postsecondary training 8
  requirements 8–9
  starting out 10
  work environment 11
computer security specialists 10
coroners 139
Cotera, Marjorie Kamys 17
Council on Forensic Science Education 19
Crick, Frances 71
Crime Investigation (Kirk) 32
crime lab directors. *See* forensic science laboratory managers
crime lab managers. *See* forensic science laboratory managers
Crime Scene Chemistry for the Armchair Sleuth (Cobb et al.) 90
crime scene investigators 15–23
  advancement 20–21
  books to read 16
  certification or licensing 19
  earnings 21

  educational requirements 18–19
  employers 20
  employment outlook 21–22
  exploring the field 20
  high school requirements 18
  history 15–16
  information 22–23
  job, described 16–18
  organizations 16, 19, 20
  postsecondary training 19
  requirements 18–20
  starting out 20
  work environment 21
crime scene technicians. *See* crime scene investigators
Crime Scene: The Ultimate Guide to Forensic Science (Platt) 165
Criminalistics: An Introduction to Forensic Science (Saferstein) 28
criminalists 24–34
  advancement 28–29
  certification or licensing 27
  earnings 29
  educational requirements 26–27
  employers 28
  employment outlook 29–30
  exploring the field 28
  high school requirements 26
  history 24–25
  information 30–31
  interview 31–34
  job, described 25–26
  organizations 27, 28
  postsecondary training 27
  requirements 26–27
  starting out 28
  work environment 29
CSI (TV show) 16
CSI Web Adventures 20
cyber examiners. *See* computer forensics specialists

D

d'Arbois, Bergeret 110
decline, explained 3
Dee Bridge (England) 98
Deloitte Touche Tohmatsu 57
Demelle, François 189
dentists 126. *See also* forensic odontologists
department chair 163
Detecting Forgery: Forensic Investigation of Documents 194
Dictionary of Occupational Titles (DOT) 2
Disaster Mortuary Operational Response Teams 134
Discover Nursing (Web site) 121
Discover Entomology: A Hobby, A Career, A Lifetime (Entomological Society of America) 113
DNA analysis technology
  criminalists 25
  forensic biologists 71, 73, 75
  forensic chemists 87, 89, 94
  forensic odontologists 128
Drug Enforcement Administration 28
Drummond, Edward 148

Dwight, Thomas 62
Dwyer, Michael 87

E

earnings, generally 1
Earnings section, explained 3
educational requirements, explained 1
Employers section, explained 3
Encore Discovery Solutions 12–14
engineering technicians 100
engineers 97. *See also* forensic engineers
Enron Corporation Stock Certificate 193
Entomological Society of America 112, 113
entomologists 103. *See also* forensic entomologists
Environmental Protection Agency 83
Ernst & Young 57
evidence technicians. *See* crime scene investigators
Exploring section, explained 2–3

F

Faulds, Henry 35
Faune des Cadavres (Megnin) 110
FBI. *See* Federal Bureau of Investigation (FBI)
Federal Bureau of Investigation (FBI)
    Automated Fingerprint Identification System
        (AFIS) 36, 38
    CODIS (Combined DNA Index System)
        71–72
    Computer Analysis and Response Team 5
    crime lab, first 70
    criminalists 25, 28, 29
    FBI: All About Fingerprints (Web site) 39
    fingerprint analysts 36, 38, 39
    forensic biologists 70, 71
    forensic botanists 80
    forensic chemists 90
    forensic entomologists 113
    forensic science laboratory managers 171
    founding of 25
    Handbook of Forensic Services 80
    Identification Division 36
    Integrated Automated Fingerprint
        Identification System 36, 38
    Magnetic Media Program 5
Ferguson's *Encyclopedia of Careers and
    Vocational Guidance* 2
Fetterolf, Monty L. 90
fingerprint analysts 35–42
    advancement 40
    certification or licensing 39
    earnings 40–41
    educational requirements 38–39
    employers 40
    employment outlook 41
    exploring the field 39
    high school requirements 38
    history 35–36
    information 41–42
    job, described 36–38
    organizations 38, 39
    postsecondary training 38–39
    requirements 38–39
    starting out 40
    work environment 40
Fingerprints (Galton) 36

Fingerprints: Analysis and Understanding
    (Hawthorne) 39
fire investigators 43–50
    advancement 48
    certification or licensing 46
    earnings 48
    educational requirements 45–46
    employers 47
    employment outlook 49
    exploring the field 47
    facts regarding 44
    high school requirements 45
    history 43
    information 49–50
    job, described 43–44
    organizations 44, 46–48
    postsecondary training 45–46
    requirements 45–47
    starting out 47–48
    work environment 48–49
fire marshals. *See* fire investigators
FNEs. *See* forensic nurse examiners (FNEs)
Food and Drug Administration 141
forensic accountants and auditors 51–61
    advancement 58
    areas of investigation 54
    certification or licensing 55–56
    earnings 58–59
    educational requirements 54–55
    employers 57
    employment outlook 60
    exploring the field 56–57
    high school requirements 54–55
    history 51–52
    information 60–61
    job, described 52–54
    organizations 55, 56, 58, 60
    postsecondary training 55
    requirements 54–56
    starting out 57
    work environment 59–60
forensic anthropologists 62–69
    advancement 68
    certification or licensing 65–66
    earnings 68–69
    educational requirements 64–65
    employers 66
    employment outlook 68–69
    exploring the field 66
    high school requirements 64–65
    history 62–63
    information 69
    job, described 63–64
    organizations 65, 67
    postsecondary training 65
    requirements 64–66
    starting out 66–67
    work environment 68
forensic biologists 70–78
    advancement 75
    certification or licensing 73
    earnings 75
    educational requirements 72–73
    employers 74
    employment outlook 76

exploring the field 74
high school requirements 72
history 70–71
information 76–78
job, described 71–72
organizations 73
postsecondary training 72–73
requirements 72–73
starting out 74–75
work environment 75–76
forensic botanists 79–85
advancement 83–84
certification or licensing 82
earnings 84
educational requirements 81–82
employers 83
employment outlook 84–85
exploring the field 82
high school requirements 81
history 79–80
information 85
job, described 80–81
organizations 80, 82, 83
postsecondary training 81–82
requirements 81–82
starting out 83
work environment 84
forensic chemists 86–96
advancement 91–92
certification or licensing 89
earnings 92
educational requirements 88–89
employers 90–91
employment outlook 93
exploring the field 90
forensic drug analysts 88
forensic drug chemists 88
high school requirements 88
history 86–87
information 93–94
interview 94–96
job, described 87–88
organizations 89
postsecondary training 88–89
requirements 88–90
starting out 91
work environment 92
Forensic Dentistry Online (Web site) 130
forensic dentists. *See* forensic odontologists
Forensic Document Examination: Principles and Practice (Koppenhaver) 194
Forensic Document Examination Technique (Vastrick) 194
forensic documents examiners. *See* questioned documents examiners
forensic drug analysts 88
forensic drug chemists 88
forensic engineers 97–108
advancement 103–104
certification or licensing 101
earnings 104
educational requirements 100–101
employers 102–103
employment outlook 104–105
engineering technicians 100

exploring the field 102
high school requirements 100–101
history 97–98
information 105–108
job, described 98–100
organizations 101–103
postsecondary training 100–101
requirements 100–102
starting out 103
technologists 100
traffic accident investigators 99–100
work environment 104
forensic entomologists 64, 109–115
advancement 113–114
certification or licensing 112
earnings 114
educational requirements 111–112
employers 113
employment outlook 114–115
exploring the field 112–113
high school requirements 111
history 109–110
information 115
job, described 110–111
organizations 112–113
postsecondary training 111–112
requirements 111–112
starting out 113
work environment 114
Forensic Examination of Digital Evidence (U.S. Department of Justice) 10
forensic investigators. *See* crime scene investigators
The Forensic Nurse (Web site) 120–121
forensic nurse examiners (FNEs) 118
forensic nurse investigators 118
forensic nurses 116–125
advancement 122
certification or licensing 120
earnings 122–123
educational requirements 119–120
employers 121–122
employment outlook 123
exploring the field 121
forensic nurse examiners (FNEs) 118
forensic nurse investigators 118
high school requirements 119
history 116–117
information 123–125
job, described 117–119
legal nurse consultants (LNCs) 118
organizations 117, 119–120
postsecondary training 119–120
requirements 119–121
sexual assault examiners (SAEs) 118
sexual assault forensic examiners (SAFEs) 118
sexual assault nurse examiners (SANEs) 118
sexual assault nurse examiners for pediatrics and adolescent populations (SANE-P) 120
sexual assault nurse examiners of adults and adolescents (SANE-A) 120
starting out 122
trauma forensic nurses 118
work environment 123

Forensic Nurse: The New Role of the Nurse in Law Enforcement (Stevens) 121
forensic odontologists 126–135
    advancement 131
    certification or licensing 129
    earnings 131
    educational requirements 128–129
    employers 130
    employment outlook 132
    exploring the field 130
    high school requirements 128
    history 126–127
    information 132–133
    interview 133–135
    job, described 127–128
    organizations 128–129, 133, 135
    postsecondary training 128–129
    requirements 128–130
    starting out 130–131
    work environment 131
forensic pathologists 136–146
    advancement 141
    certification or licensing 140
    clinical forensic pathologists 139
    coroners 139
    earnings 141
    educational requirements 139–140
    employers 140–141
    employment outlook 142
    exploring the field 140
    high school requirements 139
    history 136–137
    information 142–143
    interview 144–146
    job, described 137–139
    medical examiners 139
    medicolegal death investigators 139
    organizations 140
    postsecondary training 139–140
    requirements 139–140
    starting out 141
    work environment 142
forensic psychiatrists and psychologists 147–159
    advancement 154–155
    certification or licensing 152–153
    earnings 155
    educational requirements 151–152
    employers 154
    employment outlook 156
    exploring the field 153–154
    high school requirements 151
    history 147–149
    information 156–159
    job, described 149–150
    organizations 148, 149, 151–154
    postsecondary training 151–152
    psychiatrists, described 150
    psychologists, described 149–150
    requirements 151–153
    starting out 154
    work environment 155–156
forensic science educators 160–170
    advancement 167
    certification or licensing 164

    department chair 163
    earnings 167–168
    educational requirements 163–164
    employers 166
    employment outlook 168–169
    exploring the field 165–166
    graduate assistants 163
    high school requirements 163
    history 160–161
    information 169–170
    job, described 161–163
    organizations 164, 166
    postsecondary level, job described 161–163
    postsecondary training 163–164
    requirements 163–165
    secondary level, job described 161
    starting out 166
    work environment 168
Forensic Science for High School Students (Funkhouser) 28, 165
Forensic Science: Fundamentals and Investigations (Bertino) 28
forensic science laboratory directors. *See* forensic science laboratory managers
forensic science laboratory managers 171–180
    advancement 175
    certification or licensing 174
    earnings 175–176
    educational requirements 173
    employers 175
    employment outlook 176
    exploring the field 174–175
    high school requirements 173
    history 171
    information 176–177
    interview 177–180
    job, described 172–173
    organizations 171, 173, 175, 177–180
    postsecondary training 173
    requirements 173–174
    starting out 175
    work environment 176
forensic science technicians. *See* crime scene investigators
Forensic Science Timeline (Web site) 70, 160, 189
forensic toxicologists 181–188
    advancement 185–186
    books to read 183
    certification or licensing 184
    earnings 186
    educational requirements 183–184
    employers 185
    employment outlook 187
    exploring the field 185
    high school requirements 183
    history 181
    information 187–188
    job, described 182–183
    organizations 184, 185
    postsecondary training 184
    requirements 183–184
    starting out 185
    work environment 186–187
Forest Products Laboratory 79–80
For More Information section, explained 3

Franklin University 55
Fraud Museum 193
Freeman, Adam 133–135
French Letter 193
Friedrich, Christian 87
Frozen Sections of a Child (Dwight) 62
Fundamentals of Forensic Science (Houck and Siegel) 165
Funkhouser, John 28, 165
Future Nurses programs 121

G

Gacy, John Wayne 64
Galton, Sir Francis 36
Gialamas, Dean 177–180
Giblin, Joe 45
Goldsmith, Jack G. 90
Goldstein, Alan M. 148
graduate assistants 163
growth, explained 3
Guide for Occupational Exploration (GOE) 2
Gunn, Alan 74
Guttmacher, Manfred 149

H

Hahnemann, Samuel 87
Handbook of Fingerprint Recognition (Maltoni, et al.) 39
Handbook of Forensic Services (FBI) 80
Handbook of Psychology: Volume 11: Forensic Psychology (Goldstein) 148
handwriting identification experts. *See* questioned documents examiners
Harvard College 62
Harvard Medical School 62
Hauptmann, Bruno Richard 80
Hawthorne, Mark R. 39
Heiser, Jay G. 10
Helber, Steve 7
Hells Angels 95
Herschel, William James 35–36
High Technology Crime Investigation Association 8
The History of Fingerprints (Web site) 39
History section, explained 2
Houck, Max M. 165
Howard, John 144–146
Human Resources Development Canada 2
Hurricane Katrina 127

I

I-35W Bridge (Minnesota) 99
IAFN. *See* International Association of Forensic Nurses (IAFN)
Identification Division of the FBI 36
information on, explained 3
Inman, Keith 70, 160, 189
Internal Revenue Service (IRS) 57
International Association for Identification
    crime scene investigators 16
    criminalists 27
    fingerprint analysts 39
    forensic chemists 89

International Association of Arson Investigators 46, 48
International Association of Computer Investigative Specialists 8
International Association of Forensic Nurses (IAFN) 117, 120, 122
International Crime Scene Investigators Association 20
International High Technology Crime Investigation Association 10
International Journal of Forensic Science 162
International Organization on Computer Evidence 6
International Society of Forensic Computer Examiners 9
Intersociety Council for Pathology Information 140
interviews
    computer forensics specialists 12–14
    criminalists 31–34
    forensic chemists 94–96
    forensic odontologists 133–135
    forensic pathologists 144–146
    forensic science laboratory managers 177–180
investigative accountants. *See* forensic accountants and auditors
investigative auditors. *See* forensic accountants and auditors
IRS. *See* Internal Revenue Service (IRS)

J

Jain, Anil K. 39
JETS. *See* Junior Engineering Technical Society (JETS)
JIST Works 2
The Job section, explained 2
Joint POW/MIA Accounting Command 63
Jones, Tim 127
The Journal of Forensic Science 162
Junior Engineering Technical Society (JETS) 102

K

Katrina (Hurricane) 127
Kirk, Paul 32
Koch, Robert 136
Koehler, Arthur 79–80
Komarinski, Peter 39
Koppenhaver, Katherine M. 194
KPMG International 57
Kruse, Warren G. 9–10, 12–14

L

Lausanne, University of 160
Lausanne Institute of Police Science 160
legal nurse consultants (LNCs) 118
Lindbergh, Charles 70–71, 79–80
Linnaeus, Carolus 79
LNCs. *See* legal nurse consultants (LNCs)
Locard, Edmund 171
Lovering, Daniel 37
Lyons, University of 70, 171

M

Magnetic Media Program of FBI 5
Maio, Dario 39
Malpighi, Marcello 35
Maltoni, Davide 39
Manual of Forensic Odontology 135
Marsh, James 86–87, 181–182
Marsh Test 182
Maucieri, Louis 94–96
McNaughton, Daniel 148–149
McNaughton Rules 149
medical entomologists. *See* forensic
    entomologists
medical examiners 139
Medical School Admissions Requirements 152
medicocriminal entomologists. *See* forensic
    entomologists
medicolegal death investigators 139
Megnin, Jean Pierre 110
Menninger, Karl Augustus 149
Mental Health America 153
Minnesota, University of
    School of Nursing 117
Moorehead, Wayne 31–34
Morgagni, Giovanni Batista 136
Mount Marty College 55
Munsterberg, Hugo 147
Myers University 55

N

NAFA. *See* National Association of Forensic
    Accountants (NAFA)
NAME. *See* National Association of Medical
    Examiners (NAME)
National Aeronautics and Space Administration
    83, 103
National Association of Arson Investigators 46, 48
National Association of Colleges and Employers
    58, 84
National Association of Forensic Accountants
    (NAFA) 56, 59, 60
National Association of Medical Examiners
    (NAME) 140, 141, 144–146
National Board Dental Examinations 129
National Council of Examiners for Engineering
    and Surveying 101
National Disaster Medical Service 134
National Fire Academy 46, 47
National Fire Protection Association 44
National Institute of Standards and Technology 92
National Institutes of Health 141
National Occupational Classification (NOC)
    Index 2
National Park Service 113
Nickell, Joe 194
Nightingale, Florence 116
nurses. *See* forensic nurses
Nursing Net (Web site) 121
Nursing World (Web site) 121

O

Occupational Information Network (O*NET)-
    Standard Occupational Classification System
    (SOC) index 2

Occupational Outlook Handbook 3, 142
On the Witness Stand (Munsterberg) 147
Opportunities in Forensic Science (Camenson) 165
Orange County (California) Sheriff's Department
    177–180
Orfila, Mathieu 181
Osborn, Albert S. 189–190
Outlook section, explained 3
Overview section, explained 2

P

Pacioli, Luca 51
Pasteur, Louis 136
Pemoni, Lucy 63
Physicians Search 155
Platt, Richard 165
Prabhakar, Salil 39
PricewaterhouseCoopers 57
The Problem of Proof (Osborn) 189
psychiatrists. *See* forensic psychiatrists and
    psychologists
psychologists. *See* forensic psychiatrists and
    psychologists
Purkinie, Jan 35

Q

questioned document examiners 189–196
    advancement 194
    certification or licensing 192
    earnings 194–195
    educational requirements 192
    employers 194
    employment outlook 195
    exploring the field 193–194
    high school requirements 192
    history 189–190
    information 195–196
    organizations 189, 192–194
    postsecondary training 192
    requirements 192–193
    starting out 194
    work environment 195
Questioned Documents (Osborn) 189
Quick Facts section 2
Quintilian 15

R

Red Cross 121
Redi, Francesco L. 110
Reiss, R. A. 160
Requirements section, explained 2
Revere, Paul 125
Ridges and Furrows (Web site) 39
Robert Half International 58
Roque, Pat 172
Royal Engineers 98
Rudin, Norah 70, 160, 189

S

SAEs. *See* sexual assault examiners (SAEs)
Saferstein, Richard 28
SAFEs. *See* sexual assault forensic examiners
    (SAFEs)
Salary.com 141

SANE-A. *See* sexual assault nurse examiners of adults and adolescents (SANE-A)

SANE-P. *See* sexual assault nurse examiners for pediatrics and adolescent populations (SANE-P)

SANEs. *See* sexual assault nurse examiners (SANEs)

Sean, David 133

Secret Service 28

sexual assault examiners (SAEs) 118

sexual assault forensic examiners (SAFEs) 118

sexual assault nurse examiners (SANEs) 118

sexual assault nurse examiners for pediatrics and adolescent populations (SANE-P) 120

sexual assault nurse examiners of adults and adolescents (SANE-A) 120

Sexual Assault Resource Service 117

Siegel, Jay A. 165

Simpson, Cedric Keith 127

Socha-Gelbmann Electronic Discovery Survey 13

Society of Forensic Toxicology 185

Society of Toxicology 185, 186

Song Ci (Sung Tz'u) 109–110

Southeastern Association of Forensic Document Examiners 193

Start Here, Go Places in Business and Accounting (Web site) 3

Starting Out section, explained 3

State of New Jersey v. Bruno Richard Hauptmann 80

Stevens, Serita 121

T

teachers 160. *See also* forensic science educators

technologists 100

Teichmann, Ludwig 70

terrorist attacks of September 11, 2001 98–99, 127

Towlen, Jason 138

toxicologists 181. *See also* forensic toxicologists

traffic accident investigators 99–100

trauma forensic nurses 118

Tsunami (Asia 2004) 127

typewriting identification experts. *See* questioned documents examiners

U

U.S. Bureau of Alcohol, Tobacco, Firearms and Explosives
  criminalists 28
  fire investigators 47
  forensic chemists 88

U.S. Bureau of Labor Statistics 3

U.S. Department of Agriculture
  forensic biologists 83
  forensic chemists 91
  forensic engineers 103

U.S. Department of Defense 103

U.S. Department of Energy 92, 103

U.S. Department of Health and Human Services 92

U.S. Department of Homeland Security 103

U.S. Department of Homeland Transportation 103

U.S. Department of Justice
  Forensic Examination of Digital Evidence 10

U.S. Department of Labor
  computer forensics specialists 11
  crime scene investigators 21
  fingerprint analysts 40, 41
  fire investigators 48, 49
  forensic accountants and auditors 58, 60
  forensic anthropologists 67–69
  forensic biologists 75, 76
  forensic botanists 84
  forensic chemists 92, 93
  forensic engineers 104–105
  forensic entomologists 114
  forensic nurses 122, 123
  forensic odontologists 131, 132
  forensic psychiatrists and psychologists 155, 156
  forensic science educators 167–168
  forensic science laboratory managers 175–176
  forensic toxicologists 186
  generally 1–2
  questioned documents examiners 194–195

USDL. *See* U.S. Department of Labor

USFA. *See* U.S. Fire Administration (USFA)

U.S. Federal Computer Fraud and Abuse Act (1984) 5

U.S. Fire Administration (USFA) 47

U.S. Fish and Wildlife Service 28, 113

U.S. Forest Service 47, 80

U.S. National Library of Medicine 136–137

U.S. Postal Service 28

U.S. Public Health Service 83, 131

V

Vastrick, Thomas W. 194

Virchow, Rudolf 136

Virginia State Police Computer Evidence Recovery Unit 7

Volmar, August 171

Volonino, Linda 9

Vucetich, Juan 36

W

Wakley Thomas 136

Warren Museum of Anatomy 62

The Washing Away of Wrongs (Song Ci) 15, 110

Watson, James 71

Waynesburg College 55

Webster, John White 125–126

White, William Alanson 149

Wilkins, Maurice 71

Work Environment section, explained 3

World Trade Center terrorist attacks (2001) 98–99, 127

ML   11/10